Too often, we confuse "boy, I'm really busy," with "gee, my business is doing great!" In business, as in life, having a lot on your plate doesn't mean that you're following the healthiest path. Richardson provides practical advice businesses can use to maintain (or regain) their health. I'm going to keep this book and do regular check ups on my own.

Mary Jane Saunders
Attorney, Subway

In a sea of self-help business books, *How Fit is Your Business* provides a unique perspective on business health and vitality. The book is complete with useful tips, insight and sage advice.

Edward Johnson
President & CEO, Better Business Bureau

Any successful business knows that getting the fundamentals right is key. Mark's insight and advice on how to strengthen a business is applicable for an organization of any size and in any market. It is a valuable tool for owners and managers, providing comprehensive information about business health in an easy-to-read and actionable format.

Bruce Christensen
Vice President, GE Money

Mark has written a great book to help us all assess the fitness of our businesses and how we can make them more fit. The collapse of companies that appeared fit and some over 100 years old are clear indicators that business fitness cannot be ignored. *How Fit is Your Business* is not a one-time read, but an excellent tool to weigh your business on a regular basis.

Phil Rea
President, R2R

Mark Richardson is certainly one of the most dynamic leaders this industry has ever seen. Incorporating real life applications from his own experiences into real life guidance is what leadership and management is built upon for successful companies. Mark graciously gives back to the industry as he transforms this guidance in a very straightforward, informative manner so that all business owners can easily test the applications of their own operations to truly understanding the health and overall wellbeing of their own companies. It is through his systematic direction that being 'fit' is within reach for all entrepreneurs!

Jarred Roy
Manager, Pella Corporation

Mark Richardson brings to the conscious level the essential questions business owners should not only be asking themselves, but answering and acting on in order to succeed.

Herbert Stanwood
Senior Designer, Case Design/Remodeling

Veteran remodeler Mark Richardson is just what the doctor ordered. Through an analogy between physical wellness and business health, he meticulously leads remodelers in a self-evaluation of their businesses, dispelling common myths along the way, and then helps them write their own fitness plan for a stronger, healthier business. A must-read if you're wondering how your business can do better.

Pat O'Toole
Editor-In Chief, *Qualified Remodeler* Magazine

This book provides a rare combination of clear and cohesive business tactics matched with actionable objectives.

Bruce Case
COO, Case Design/Remodeling

For those folks contemplating starting a business, ANY BUSINESS, this book is for you. The author explains in detail what a healthy business looks like as well as how to monitor and improve upon that health. The analogies and metaphors presented make this more than a business book with its lessons accessible to all. Buy and read this book and you'll never guess about how your business is doing. You'll know every day whether you are making decisions that bring you closer to, or further from your goals.

Stephen Scholl
AVP, Case Handyman

What an awesome easy to follow tool for any type of business owner or manager of a business. Not only does this book provide the tools to understand one's business health, but it provides the methods and solutions to improving one's business health. It's definitely an easy read that will make one pause and think, "Am I doing the right things to maximize sales and profits?"

Mike Bozick
Marketing, Henkel Corporation

How Fit Is Your Business needs to be on every entrepreneur's book-shelf and in their briefcase. Mark's years of building a national power-house company shine through in this practical and insightful book that reminds all of us of the importance of periodic and candid check-ups as a prerequisite to the health and strength of our companies.

Andrew J. Sherman
Partner, Dickstein Shapiro

Bull's eye for business success. Mark Richardson's insightful analogy between a healthy body and a healthy business gives real life, action-able direction to any business owner who wants to grow.

Steve Bursten
Founder, Exciting Windows

This book is a must-read whether your business is in goods or ser-vices. The health comparison creates clear, precise actions you can use to evaluate and improve both immediate and long term business operations, particularly in the emerging economic challenges.

Tom Regan
Dean, College of Architecture, Texas A&M University

HOW FIT IS YOUR BUSINESS?

HOW FIT IS YOUR BUSINESS?

A Complete Checkup and Prescription
for Better Business Health

Mark Richardson

Published by Elevate, Charleston, South Carolina.
Member of Advantage Media Group.

ELEVATE is a registered trademark and the
Elevate colophon is a trademark of Advantage Media Group, Inc.

Printed in the United States of America

ISBN: 978-1-60194-019-3

Library of Congress Cataloging-in-Publication Data
   Richardson, Mark G., 1955-
   How fit is your business? : a complete checkup and prescription for better business health / by Mark G. Richardson ; with Sal Alfano.
   p. cm.
   ISBN 978-1-60194-019-3
1. Management--Evaluation. 2. Business enterprises--Evaluation. I. Alfano, Salvatore. II. Title.
HD31.R4934 2008
658.4'01--dc22
                                        2008022195

FOR JESSICA, JAMIE AND BRETT

Contents

Part Three: Improving Your Business

Foreword

Although both "business" and "fitness" appear in the title of this book, it has little to do with helping you achieve good physical fitness, nor will it teach you anything about how to start up a health club. The business the title refers to is the one you're already running, and the fitness it promises is not physical health, but the health of your business.

The first time I heard Mark Richardson apply the metaphor of health and fitness to business concepts was five years ago during a presentation he gave at a one-day conference for remodeling contractors. It began, as so many of Mark's presentations do, with a series of questions for the audience.

"If I asked you to name three things that are clear markers of good physical health and well-being, what would they be?" Mark asked.

"Low cholesterol," someone quickly answered. "Normal blood pressure," someone else added; then "proper weight" from the back of the room.

Obviously pleased with both the answers and how fast the audience responded, Mark kept the momentum going with a question about the tools doctors might use to measure physical health. He quickly got more good answers: thermometer, scale, blood test, treadmill.

"What would we do if our cholesterol were too high?"

"Stop eating fatty foods."

"What about being overweight, what then?"

"Go on a diet."

"How about high blood pressure?"

"See a doctor for a prescription."

More questions; more good, quick answers. Mark had made his point: we all have a clear idea of what it means to be physically healthy, and we all know what to do to get well again if we're not in such good shape. Now he went to the heart of the matter.

"Let's think about your business," Mark began. "What three things are clear markers of good business health."

Silence. Then a barely audible "Good sales" from the back of the room. More silence. Mark looked around, and repeated the question. Someone took a guess: "Profit?" Then someone else added, "Good referrals?"

It was clear to everyone that the answers to this new question hadn't come as quickly or with the confidence of the answers about physical health. Mark had the audience right where he wanted them.

"Sales, profit, referrals—good," he repeated. "And what tools do we use to measure them?

Silence again. "Money in the bank," someone finally offered, stirring some nervous laughter. "Lots of work lined up," someone else added.

"And if our business is unhealthy, what do we do to get back on track?" Silence.

What happened in that room over the next hour was the abridged version of what you're about to read. Mark led the audience through a ten-point business fitness "checkup," asking attendees to rate themselves and their companies on each component, then explaining what the results could tell them about the health of the business. Mark's objective was to transfer the notion of physical health and fitness, something everyone in the audience knew and understood, to the way we think about business. It was a clever idea that clicked with the audience. As one of the speakers on the program, I had the opportunity to hear it many more times over the next few weeks, and it clicked with every audience.

After the speaking tour ended, I didn't think much about the business fitness checkup again until Mark mentioned it two years later over lunch at Café Deluxe in Bethesda, Md. I had been editing Mark's column for Remodeling magazine for a number of years, and we made a habit of getting together for lunch every couple of months. Through the exchange of ideas in the column and those meetings, we had come to recognize how much alike our thinking was when it came to issues affecting small businesses. In one way, this made sense because we both had connections to the remodeling business; in my case, I had been a remodeler and custom home builder for 20 years before I started editing magazines for contractors; and Mark had worked as an architectural designer before turning to business management of a remodeling firm. What was a bit surprising, however, was that we saw eye to eye on so many issues despite the fact that Mark's business was literally 100 times bigger than mine had ever been. It seemed clear to both of us that some things were true of all businesses no matter how big or small, and irrespective of the product or service that they delivered.

Soon, "the book" was on the agenda every time we met. Deciding whether or not to proceed was never a question of the topic or its timeliness, it was more a matter of figuring out how to fit it into our schedules. I'm glad we found the time because, even with all of the business books on the market, I think there are several unique things about this one.

First, a fitness checkup and prescription for business health is not merely a clever idea, it works. This isn't just my opinion. I have seen the looks on the faces of Mark's audiences when he leads the live version of this check-up. And I have talked with people who have attended Mark's presentations and used the checkup to identify and correct weaknesses in their businesses.

Second, whereas the live 60-minute version I first witnessed addressed mainly the fitness check-up, the book by virtue of its length also provides a prescription for improvement in each of the critical areas. The simple rating system is a remarkably accurate tool for diagnosing "illness" within a business, and the corresponding improvement sections of the book provide step-by-step "treatments" on how to nurse it back to health. It doesn't promise overnight miracles; in fact, the approach is deliberate and incremental. Businesses don't grow ill over night and there are no shortcuts to making them healthy again.

Finally, the process of diagnosis and prescription put forth in these pages is repeatable. It is designed to be revisited again and again as a business changes in response to internal or external forces. In fact, a central theme of this book is the importance of constantly monitoring a business's "vital signs." Business is complex, and success is a moving target. Efforts to improve in one area draw resources away from other parts of the business, and even incremental changes can have far-reaching effects.

Although Mark's business experience comes mainly from the remodeling industry, I believe the principles put forth here apply to small businesses of virtually any type. The health and fitness metaphor does the heavy lifting with regard to the overall idea of diagnosing fitness and prescribing treatment to restore health, but the main thing is the process it is used to describe. I have no doubt that anyone who makes a genuine effort to follow the step-by-step checkup and apply the suggestions for improvement will gain new insight into what makes them successful and what is holding them back from even greater success.

Sal Alfano
May, 2008
Washington, D.C.

Acknowledgements

Acknowledgements are an author's indulgence. They are personal and often obscure, and have very little to do with the average reader, at least not directly. But as I have grown older and a bit wiser, I have come to realize that our lives are a series of moments and passages, some purposeful, some accidental, but all stemming from our interaction with the people around us. Our natural inclination is to see order in chaos, to impose design on randomness; and writing an acknowledgement, I have now discovered, is as good a place to start as any. In fact, in the spirit of improving yourself and your business (which is what this book is all about), writing your own acknowledgement is the perfect way to isolate the "moments of truth" that shaped your life, and bring to mind all those who helped you along the way. In my own case, there are many.

I begin with my parents, who laid my life's foundation, one that is both solid and broad. The environment they provided offered many choices with little risk of failure or injury.

I also want to acknowledge Thomas Regan, my architecture professor and advisor at Virginia Tech and my first real mentor. Professor Regan taught me how to think. He helped me understand that architecture was only the vehicle for my life's journey, and he helped me to see things through a wider lens and to adopt a perspective that was less literal. He also showed me that that we are not so much a product of *what* we see but *how* we see, and that if we look through the right lens, there is much to see in every aspect of the world.

Fred Case has been a friend and mentor, a partner and sounding board. Fred is the ultimate opportunity maker and has created the very fertile landscape in which I have been able to flourish. When I struggled to find the next challenge to fuel my passion, Fred provided an environment in which I could conduct experiments and practice. Many of the ideas in this book spring directly from that nurturing ground and our relationship.

I want also to thank my wife, Margie. From her nurturing of our three wonderful children, to the welcoming comforts of our home, to the effortless way she removes any and all obstacles to my growth, she adds color to a life that would otherwise be black and white. We are very different personalities, but without Margie my life would be incomplete.

Many others have served as my life advisors and supporters: John Richardson, Mike Allen, Laurie Griel, Andrew Sherman, Peter Miller, and my management team at Case: Bruce Case, Bill Millholland, Jan Shaut, Mike Ethier, George Wiessgerber, Tim Walker, and Joaquin Erazo.

Thanks also to the many other friends and acquaintances who have supported me over the years and who may have offered an insight or tidbit that I unconsciously adopted or incorporated into my thinking without being aware of the source.

Finally, this book would not have been possible without my friend and writing partner, Sal Alfano. Sal makes me better. He challenges me to stretch thought muscles that would otherwise lie dormant. He has helped me to find my voice, but still adds flavor to my sometimes dry prose. He always knows what I mean regardless of what I actually say, and through his magic has brought my ideas to life for others.

Introduction

"When you look at the sun, you see no shadows "
-Helen Keller

Many years ago, while flipping through TV channels, I came across an infomercial on personal weight loss. I feel the same way about paid programming on TV as most other people—may the buyer beware!—but this program interested me for two reasons. First, the program promised a weight loss of ten pounds in twenty-one days, which struck a chord with me, because I had about fifty pounds to lose. Second, the program was designed around a methodical, easy to comprehend process, beginning with small but well-defined baby steps, and then increasing in intensity day after day. This incremental system appealed to me, so I ordered the program and began the process. The results were liberating. Not only did I lose the fifty pounds over a period of few months, I went on to participate in one-hundred-mile cycling marathons called "century rides," something I would never have considered possible. More important, I learned a technique for improvement and change that I was able to apply to other areas of my personal and business life.

My first attempt to translate this process into another part of my world was to develop and author an audio program called The 30-Day Remodeling Business Fitness Program. I guided the listener through a methodical, step-by-step process that began with taking inventory of the business, then developing plans for improvement, and finally rolling out and monitoring the changes. While this "fitness" program was well received and continues to be relevant, it was missing a key element: it didn't answer the question, "What is a fit business?" It is difficult to understand and improve on anything if you don't have a benchmark against which to measure progress. This benchmark not only allows you to look at your own history but also gives a means to compare to other businesses.

Since I had already started using the metaphor of fitness, it seemed only natural to draw the parallel between personal health and fitness, and business fitness. By connecting the dots between personal and business fitness, we remove some of the mystery from the process of improvement. We can take an aspect of our lives that we all live and breathe with every day and use it to find new but less obvious relationships and meaning in our businesses. Imagine how difficult it would be to develop a plan for weight loss and personal fitness if you did not have a clear image of what fitness meant or even some basic tools, like a scale, to measure it.

In this book, I begin by discussing why we have such a clear image of what personal fitness is but such a fuzzy picture of what business fitness is. This leads me to a breakdown of some business misconceptions that often lead us off on the wrong track. Next, I will bring you and your business into the examining room and conduct a ten-point business fitness checkup with a scoring system that will give you a foundation for a proper prescription. I will then show you how to interpret these results to establish a benchmark as a tool to measure your business and to compare it to other businesses. The ten criteria in the checkup also create a forum for determining specific areas where your business needs improvement. Finally, like any good doctor, I will set the stage for you to come back and have an annual checkup to monitor your progress.

Throughout this book, I use examples from everyday life to remove the confusion and mystery of business health and fitness. Business can be very complicated, but by breaking it down into small parts and creating a system for evaluation and improvement, I believe I can make business fitness easier to comprehend. As with our personal health and fitness, we need to have a clear image of what business health is before we can ever attempt to achieve it.

Part One:

Why a Fitness Checkup for Business?

What Is "Fit"?

*"Business is a game, the greatest game in the
world if you know how to play it"*
- Thomas Watson

If we look in the dictionary, we find that *fit* means,
"in good condition" and *health* is defined as "sound-
ness of body." These definitions are both obvious and
well understood for almost all of us. If I ask you to write
down ten attributes of a fit and healthy person, you could
do it with ease. You might begin with obvious physical attributes, like good muscle tone and proper weight. Almost
everyone would also agree that a healthy, fit person is free of
disease and shows few signs of stress. You might list observations about lifestyle, diet, and other habits that contribute
to positive health and fitness. Finally, you might look for an absence of unhealthy attributes, such as smoking or excessive drinking, to further distinguish your image of a healthy person from that of an unhealthy person.

Not only is this exercise very easy, most people would agree with
your list. The ability to distinguish good health from bad is perfectly clear
to us. We are conditioned from childhood to make black-and-white judg-

ments about physical health and fitness. In fact, we are immersed almost constantly in a barrage of information about our physical health. We are the target of cottage industries that have sprung up around diet programs and personal exercise equipment, telling us why we need to improve, and then supplying the means to make that improvement. The popular media informs us daily with stories of obesity, statistics on disease, and tales about the good or bad effects that food choices have on our health. Even our government mandates that the food industry provide proper disclosure of key nutritional metrics—fat, calories, sodium, etc.—on almost every food item we buy. Most medicines are also required to display a warning label about possible side effects or potentially unhealthy consequences.

All of these measures have combined to create a level of awareness that makes understanding physical health and fitness second nature to us. Occasionally, we receive new information that debunks some previously held belief about a particular diet or exercise regimen, such as the surprising health benefits of drinking red wine or the temporary nature of weight loss on a low carb diet. While these insights may spark our interest, they rarely undermine our basic image and understanding of what constitutes physical health and fitness.

On top of all that, we have at our fingertips many tools and tests that both provide a benchmark of our current health and also help us monitor our progress when we endeavor to get healthier and improve our fitness levels. These monitoring devices are as simple as a bathroom scale and as complex as an MRI. Imagine how difficult it would be to monitor your health without some of these basic tools. Imagine the effect on your exercise routine if you did not have easy access to a heart rate monitor or didn't know how many calories you were burning per hour. When it comes to our physical health, we take all of these tools, and all of this information and feedback for granted. They provide not just a way to simplify and understand a complex issue, they also give us a clear road map for how to improve.

We need a similar set of monitoring devices and feedback to help us benchmark the health and fitness of our businesses, and to help show us what needs to be done to improve. In the coming chapters, we will begin to construct a checkup to fill that gap. But first, we need to understand some common misconceptions about business health that may be holding us back.

Misconceptions of Business Fitness

"Whoever said, 'It's not whether you win or lose that counts,' probably lost."
- Martina Navratilova

Whether it is in our personal lives or our businesses, an incorrect belief, thinking something is good when it is not, can really throw us off course. For example, it used to be a widely held belief that fitness was simply a matter of training as hard as you could for as long as you could. "No pain, no gain" was the rallying cry, and everyone from weekend enthusiasts to professional athletes focused on training regimens that constantly ratcheted up the pressure. Today, athletes and trainers have learned that working harder is not the best way to make progress. They know that our bodies need a recovery period, and that alternating strenuous workouts with more relaxed routines sets the foundation for better results.

In the same way, there are many common misconceptions about what makes for a successful business. Erroneous beliefs about business health and fitness affect our day-to-day decisions and give us a false sense of confidence. Some of these misconceptions are small and some are large, but they all send the wrong signal and, if followed, will drive us off course. Imagine if your bathroom scale was slightly miscalibrated, and it appeared that you had lost an extra two or three pounds when in fact you had gained five. Or what if a blood test revealed a false positive for a serious disorder? Though different in severity, both of these examples would have a strong effect on your emotions, your self-image, and your decisions about what to do next.

Every industry or business category has its own pet beliefs about what constitutes a sign of good business health. Here are some that I encounter most often in the remodeling industry.

"We are booked out for six months." Over the years, I have found it interesting that many small- to medium-sized remodeling businesses gauge how well they are doing based on their backlog of work. Often when I am addressing a group of business owners and someone says he is booked out for six months or more, I ask him how it makes him feel. I have asked this question hundreds of times to a variety of audiences, and the answers I generally get are "Great," "Confident," or "Secure." But I get a very different answer when I ask the same audience to consider how a manufacturer in the same position would feel. Imagine for a moment the effect on the business of a manufacturer of windows or faucets who couldn't deliver a product to a new client for six months. It would be disastrous; the long wait for delivery would drive away even their most loyal customers.

If you believe that the longer you are booked out the better, then you are being fooled by a misconception. You may believe that things are good when, in fact, you may be losing market share. Yes, everyone ought to have a backlog—but it needs to be the right size, one that allows your process-es and systems to function properly. Too little backlog and you may find yourself scrambling for your next piece of business; too great a backlog and your customer base may disappear or change its character. Understanding what makes for the right amount of backlog is part of the process that leads to a fit business. Finding the balance and using *that* as a target is where healthy businesses want to be.

"Almost all my business comes from personal referrals." As you think about your business, how does this statement make you feel? For most of my audiences, the response is very positive. "It makes me feel proud," I hear people say, or, "This is a great way to position ourselves." While I would agree that every business benefits from personal referrals, there may be another way to think about this. When all of your business comes from personal referrals, you are not really in control of your future. If the economy slows down or a specific market changes, you need to be able to generate new clients. Over-reliance on referrals can make your marketing "muscles" weak; when you need some "heavy lifting," your strength will not be able to handle it. Most businesses with a very high percentage of revenue from personal referrals ride a rollercoaster from good times to bad. Their growth is not as sustainable as it should be, and they see only modest gains over long periods of time. Can you get the phone to ring with out depending on your existing client base?

"Our sales are up by 30 percent over last year." Imagine you are at a reception and share this news with an old friend. You're probably feeling pretty good about yourself and your team. But if I were to look behind the curtain, I doubt you would get a slap on the back from me. More businesses have imploded because of an excessively high rate of growth in sales than the reverse. Too much change too fast is unhealthy. We all know the dangers of crash diets when it comes to our personal health. Unless you are severely obese, very few health professionals would encourage you to lose five or ten pounds in a week.

Our bodies are like machines, and so are our businesses. A machine is designed to run at an optimum speed for ideal performance. If you exceed that limit, it may affect efficiency and, ultimately, life expectancy. In business, systems and processes are designed for a specific volume of sales;

checks and balances are in place to help maintain proper quality of product and service. These limits should not be exceeded by too wide a margin. The levels of investment and infrastructure should be in sync with both short- and long-term goals. Unless the business is a start-up, huge growth in sales is not generally a positive sign for health and fitness.

"We just landed the largest contract ever!" Generally, a remodeling contractor makes a statement like this with a lot of enthusiasm. Everyone dreams of "landing the big one," and when it happens, most assume that their days of struggling to get their business going are over. Occasionally, however, I get a chance to follow up with these business owners six or twelve months later, and I always make it a point to ask them how they are feeling about that home run deal. With few exceptions, the enthusiasm has been replaced with regret that they ever landed that big fish.

Often when I speak to remodeling contractors, I ask the audience about the ideal project size for their companies. Usually, the answers range from "It doesn't matter" to "The bigger the better." Sometimes, though, someone will shout out a specific number, like $72,500. The audience usu- ally reacts with nervous laughter, but then it begins to sink in. Whereas most remodelers believe that if they are competent to do small projects then they should be equally equipped to do large projects, and vice versa, I believe that there is a sweet spot in business—and, more importantly, that knowledge of what that sweet spot is should guide business decisions.

If you believe "bigger is better" or "size doesn't matter," then you may be misguided. Distractions or false hopes in business can lead to more problems than solutions.

"We are very busy." Even though most business owners today do not equate being busy with success, it would be remiss not to highlight this misconception because people in certain roles are particularly susceptible to it. It may be, for example, that a change in market conditions or the overall selling environment is keeping salespeople busier than ever chasing

down new clients or spending more time than ever as "unpaid consultants" or "professional researchers" for prospective customers. Although they feel like they are making progress, when you analyze a typical day in their lives, you realize that they are spending more hours getting less accomplished. This same dynamic commonly occurs in people with management and client support responsibilities. They may be moving at a frenetic pace, spending more time than usual "putting out fires," but all of this activity contributes nothing to the company's success and often works against it.

Activity is often mistaken as a sign of good business health. When we feel busy, it's easy to assume that we are moving the enterprise forward. After all, no one wants to be the Maytag man. We all want to believe that what we are doing is important and meaningful. Being busy does that, but it is not necessarily a positive sign of health.

Every business owner can, with a little reflection, come up with more examples like these. Why is it that so many of the commonsense observations we make about our business health and fitness are so far from the mark? More importantly, what observations should we be making to get a true picture of where our businesses are strong and where they need improvement?

Business Blindness

B y now, some of you are starting to feel a little uneasy. We haven't yet reached the actual fitness checkup, but already you are beginning to question your assumptions about the health of your business or are at least curious about what business fitness means. These beliefs have been guiding you for years, but now uncertainty has begun to creep in. "Why did I not think about this before?" you might be asking yourself and, "How much time have I been wasting on the wrong stuff?"

Recognizing the need for improvement rarely occurs gradually; more often it begins with a wake-up call. With regard to our personal health, if we're lucky it may come in the form of a test result; if we're unlucky or have ignored or been unaware of the symptoms for too long, it may manifest itself in something more serious, like a heart attack or stroke. In the same way, if we ignore the symptoms of an unhealthy business for too long, the bad news may come from our accountant or banker or, worse, from our customers. Fortunately, it also can also come in a more constructive way, like the checkup in this book.

Still, the question remains: why are most businesspeople blind to the issues of business health? It is not a casual question, especially when you consider some of the statistics relating to business failure. According to the Small Business Administration, three out of five businesses close their doors within the first five years; about nine out of ten are out of business within ten years. These are terrible odds. Would you ever board a plane if there were a 60 percent chance it would crash? Would you invest in real estate if after ten years there were a 90 percent chance of foreclosure?

Businesspeople who take these levels of risk seriously tend to make the subject of business acumen and fitness a top priority. Given the pain that business failure causes, few business owners would reject a chance to turn back the clock and either approach their businesses differently or possibly opt not to launch a business at all.

Why are businesspeople blind to the issues of business fitness and health? I think there are several reasons.

A natural business. The first reason has to do with the motivation for starting a business in the first place. When you ask most business owners what their passion was in the early days of their businesses, most point to the craft, the product, or the service of the business, not business itself. In the business I know best, home remodeling, most practitioners got started because they loved to build things or they had a knack for solving problems and enjoyed talking with homeowners about their homes. These kinds of skills and enthusiasm may very well be essential to selling and delivering a particular product or service, but they do not guarantee good business health.

And the problem tends to grow worse over time. My observations of businesspeople over the years reveal that most of them prefer to invest more and more time in getting better at the "natural" set of skills that are responsible for their early success, ignoring other critical business skills that don't really interest them. This creates an imbalance that can conceal the signs of impending failure. A business owner who focuses only on what he or she is good at or has a passion for will feel fulfilled and will most likely extend this positive feeling to the business itself. But lacking the tools required to evaluate business performance—or at least lacking an interest in mastering and using those tools—actually contributes to the downfall of the business, and the owner is likely to be completely blindsided when it happens.

Business by accident. A second reason owners ignore business fundamentals is that businesses tend to start, grow, and develop by accident, not by design. Most business owners start by putting a toe in the water and don't get serious about it until the flood-level has risen to their chest. Over the years, I have asked many people attending my business seminars if they have a written business plan, and consistently fewer than five percent of attendees raise their hands. And these people are typically owners of businesses that are between five and twenty years old.

This phenomenon is not confined to businesses like home remodeling, which has low barriers to entry. Doctors, dentists, lawyers, engineers, and other professionals required to obtain advanced degrees and licensing are also susceptible. Most of the training for these professions has to do with gaining the skills required to deliver the product or service, not with managing the business itself. The architecture school I attended did a good job of ensuring its graduates were competent designers but offered virtually nothing to ensure they would become successful businesspeople. In fact, many of the professors treated any discussion about business strategies as irrelevant and even contradictory to their mission as educators. Even business school curriculums focus more on theoretical aspects of business and less on the fundamentals of how to actually run a successful company.

Easy entry. The third reason business owners are ignorant of or naive about factors that affect a business's health and fitness is that getting into business is generally easy. In most cases, not much upfront capital is required, and there are few regulatory hoops to jump through beyond presenting a valid driver's license. As the joke goes in the remodeling business, you also need a ladder and a dog. Virtually anyone can start a business without obtaining any training or certifications and without being subjected to business proficiency testing.

I am certainly not an advocate of heavy governmental controls in private business, nor am I suggesting the American dream should be tied up in a lot of red tape. I am suggesting, however, that the price we pay for unfettered entry into the business community is a good number of misguided, unhealthy businesses. Unfortunately, the consumer is often the victim of this system—but not the only victim. Strong, well-run companies are often painted with the same brush as those that fail miserably, and the result in some cases is a tarnished reputation for an entire industry.

Business is a game. To win, you need to understand the rules, master the language, and develop successful strategies. If you are operating your business based on false assumptions, or if you are not evaluating it with the proper criteria, then any success you have enjoyed up until now is merely a happy coincidence.

Introduction to the Checkup

"The future ain't what it used to be"

- Yogi Berra

As we have discussed in previous chapters, personal health and fitness is something we can easily recognize. We also have little difficulty naming specific ways we can measure our physical health. We all understand that we can see some signs of health with the naked eye but that others require complex testing. All of these pieces fit together to form our image of what it means to be healthy. Consciously or not, we constantly monitor our health, and in most cases we can easily tell when our level of fitness has dropped.

I have chosen deliberately to present a business fitness test in the familiar form of a personal physical checkup. The more closely you can follow that parallel process, the more you will gain from this exercise. You know, for example, that the results of a physical exam will not be as helpful if you skip any of the steps. The same is true of this business checkup. It is a process and a system that should be followed step by step. I will offer plenty of guidance along the way, but you are your own proctor. The more honest you are with your answers, the more useful the results of the checkup will be.

In the checkup itself, each business fitness element is weighted equally, and you will be asked to rate each one. The scoring system is simple: the scale ranges from 1 on the low side to 10 as the maximum. Fractional scores are okay, too; recording a 7.5 after some serious reflection is better than rounding up to 8 or down to 7 just for the sake of using round numbers.

When you reach the end of the checkup, you will have recorded ten scores, one for each of the ten fitness criteria. Although the scores are subjective, I have found that they produce consistent results. A score of 10 indicates that your business is performing at its peak. Use a score of 10 if you feel you are far above your competition in the relevant area and there is little or no room for improvement.

A score of 5 indicates average performance—like earning a grade of "C" in school. An element scored with a 5 may not be causing you much pain at the moment, but it represents an opportunity for improvement. Moving from a score of 5 to a score of 6 or 7 would clearly create a more positive picture.

A score of 1 means that this aspect of your business is critically ill and improving performance should move to the top of your to-do list. The good news is that efforts to improve a score of 1 often show quick results because there is nowhere to go but up. It's much easier to move a score of 1 to a score of 2 or 3 than it is to move an 8 to a 9.

Each chapter explains the fitness criteria in terms you can easily recognize in your particular business. You still need to read carefully, however, because my experience is that much of what you will read is new information. Or at least it represents a new way of thinking about your business. On the other hand, while unfamiliar material may appeal to you most, it would be a mistake to ignore sections in which the subject matter seems too basic. It is in just these areas that you are more likely to uncover false assumptions or discover new ways of thinking about familiar issues. Remember, too, that although each chapter is designed to be read independently and scored separately, they are like the pieces of a jigsaw puzzle; there is real benefit in looking at each piece in relation to all of the others.

There are no "right" answers in this fitness checkup, and researching and gathering data will not help your results. Adopting a balanced frame of mind, however, will make a difference. It is human nature to look into the mirror and exaggerate what you see, for better or worse. So if you are going through a personal or professional crisis, either check those issues at the door before diving into this checkup or postpone the checkup until some of the turmoil has been resolved. If you have many distractions that could make it difficult to focus, try to isolate yourself from e-mail or cell phone access for a couple of hours to concentrate on the task at hand.

Pace and timing are also important to the outcome of this checkup. Some may find it beneficial to read through all of the checkup sections, and then go back to each one to record a score. Others may prefer to score themselves the first time through. No single approach works better than any other, so try to find what works for you. Remember, too, that you can return again and again to repeat the checkup. In fact, it is my hope that the results will be so useful and you will see such improvement that you will make it a regular practice to take the test and analyze your score, just like an annual physical.

This checkup is a personal process, and you may want your scores to remain private. I do recommend, however, that after you have taken this test, you give a fitness book to some of your key team members or to your spouse. They will have insights about your business that only their unique perspective can generate. Plus, their direct participation in the checkup will make it easier to implement any improvements that the test reveals are needed. Again, you will get more valuable information if you let the book speak for itself and avoid guiding or influencing team members' scoring.

With all of this talk of scores and results, it is easy to lose sight of the fact that the whole purpose is to have a meaningful experience, one that is both a journey and a destination. Although the goal is to end up with an overall score for your business fitness, the process of thinking about the criteria and evaluating how your company measures up is equally valuable, if not more important. Regardless of how you score yourself, the checkup itself should get the wheels turning on ways you can improve.

Finally, while it is important to avoid being too casual in your approach to this checkup, you should also guard against becoming too obsessed. Make this checkup meaningful, and make it a positive tool for your business, but also make it fun. Business is a game—a difficult one, but a game nonetheless. You will play the game better if you are having fun.

Part Two:

The Business Fitness Checkup

Knowing Your Numbers

"If it doesn't matter who wins or loses, then why do we keep score?"
-Vince Lombardi

When it comes to personal health and fitness, we can measure vital statistics in a variety of ways. Some, such as weight or basic stamina, are pretty obvious from causal observation. Others, such as blood pressure and cholesterol levels require simple testing by your doctor to determine whether or not you are within healthy ranges. More complicated, targeted testing may be required if you or your doctor has a particular concern or if you have reached a certain age.

Measurements like these are useful to anyone concerned about remaining reasonably healthy. But to a person committed to moving beyond average health and achieving a higher level of fitness, these kinds of metrics are even more compelling. A person committed to fitness will focus on these vital statistics not only to establish a baseline and monitor progress, but also to create a plan for diet and exercise.

Like your personal health, your business also has vital statistics. And as is true of health metrics, some aspects of your business are easier to measure than others. Early in your journey to better business fitness, pay attention to the obvious numbers first. Then, as you improve, you can begin to use more complicated diagnostic tools to measure other critical business functions.

As you reflect on the various ways that numbers relate to business fitness, you might notice that one obvious success measurement is missing— profitability. I'll treat this critical element in a separate chapter later on, so be patient and stick to the checkup process.

Vital numbers. All businesses have certain numbers that are essential to monitor. Retailers know, for example, that the average spend per customer is an important benchmark to watch, while in food services, managers keep an eye on the number of seatings during a specific time period. In the remodeling business, the most important numbers to monitor are total sales, gross profit margin (percentage and dollars), overhead expense, and percentage of completion. More sophisticated remodeling companies will also watch the number of inquiries or leads, the cost per lead, sales close rates, and average project size.

If numbers like these are checked frequently enough, even slight fluctuations can impart valuable intelligence about how a business is performing. More importantly, these measurements serve as an early warning system that gives managers and owners enough time to make adjustments.

Knowing what to monitor is only half the battle. The real work comes with creating and managing the systems that deliver the critical statistics at regular intervals. Owners of small businesses should be able to keep the most vital numbers in their heads, but all business owners should have their company's vital numbers at their fingertips.

How do you measure up? Do you know which parts of your business you should be monitoring? Do you have ways to gather critical statistics weekly, monthly, quarterly, or annually as required? Can you recite your company's vital numbers without having to look them up? If you had to look them up, would you know where to find them or would you have to ask the bookkeeper?

Guided by numbers. Knowing your company's critical numbers is only the first step; more important is what you do with this knowledge. If you are on a diet, knowing that you gained two pounds after a holiday feast is only useful if it prompts you to push away from the table the next day; it helps you reach your weight loss goal only if it spurs you to increase your exercise for a couple of days and have the discipline to check your weight again a week later.

In the same way, knowing your numbers is only useful if it leads to change and re-measurement. In my studies of business behavior, I find that the difference between knowing and acting on what you know is often what separates average businesses from great ones. In today's business environment, it's easy to become overwhelmed with the number of balls you have to keep in the air. That makes it difficult to make room for review of key metrics in your daily routine. Most business owners focus attention on the business's vital signs only when symptoms of illness are impossible to ignore, but by then it is very tough to get on the road to recovery. Owners of healthy businesses have mastered the discipline of including vital statistics into their day-to-day decision-making process.

Knowing your numbers also keeps you grounded in reality. Our emotional ups and downs play games with our perceptions and can affect our ability to evaluate accurately how we are performing. We may exaggerate a small failure into an attitude of defeat that holds us back from reaching our goals. Or our exhilaration over our success may lead us into arrogance or complacency. Understanding key metrics enables business owners to set goals they know they can achieve without too much risk.

Do you communicate critical business metrics to all members of your organization? Are critical statistics discussed regularly at staff meetings? Do team members at all levels rely on metrics as a basis for action?

Regular review. If you're trying to lose weight, you might climb onto a scale more often than someone whose weight is at an optimal level. But some frequency intervals make more sense than others. Weighing yourself every hour would be foolish because the variance from one measurement to the next would be so small. Monitoring your weight daily might be okay if you were seriously overweight because a daily weigh-in would show some progress. Otherwise, however, too short an interval might send false signals about how well your diet or exercise regimen is working. Weekly monitoring is probably ideal in the early stages, increasing to monthly as you come closer to your weight goal. These frequency intervals would give you measurable results that allow for simple adjustments to help you stay on track without overreacting.

What's good for a weight loss program is also good for your business. Reviewing your numbers regularly is essential if you want to take your business to a higher level. It is not a matter of being more intelligent than other business owners, it is about having the discipline to work smart. Most successful business leaders put a priority on making these kinds of activities into success habits. A "success habit" is an activity or way of thinking that not only contributes to a positive outcome but also does so because, through repetition and practice, it has become second nature. For example, most good pilots have trained themselves to check altitude, air speed, weather patterns, fuel levels, and other gauges on their instrument panel every few minutes without having to think deliberately about it.

New Year's resolutions work—or fail to work—for the same reason. Most people who make New Year's resolutions in January fall off the wagon by February or March. Rarely does this happen because the resolutions were unrealistic or stupid, or because the behavior of others interfered. Resolutions are broken because most people don't monitor their progress, so the resolution never becomes a success habit. By the time they realize they have drifted off course, the pain of getting back on target is too great, so they quit trying.

What is the right monitoring cycle for key business indicators? It depends, not only on your product or service, but also on your present business health. For example, if you are in a service business that bills clients at an hourly rate, you might want to take the pulse on billings once a day, or at least once a week. If, on the other hand, your business involves larger contracts, such as real estate transactions or construction projects, the appropriate monitoring cycle may be monthly or even quarterly.

The important question for this business fitness element is this: do you have a review cycle for your important business metrics and does that review actually take place?

Financial tools. If you didn't know how to use a scale, it would be tough to monitor your weight. If you weren't able to make any sense out of the information on the food labels at the grocery store, then it would be difficult to make good buying decisions to prepare balanced meals.

Your business has some standard financial tools, too. These tools not only help you to understand the health and fitness of your business, they also allow an objective observer from outside your business to guide and advise you.

The most basic financial tools are your profit and loss statement and your balance sheet. Understanding these reports doesn't mean you have to know how to prepare them; it just means you are conversant enough with them to make sound judgments based on the information they hold. I don't understand how a nutritionist determines the percentage of fat in certain foods, but I do understand how to read food labels. I know how much fat is too much, and based on that I can make a judgment about which foods to consume. Similarly, I don't need to know how a digital scale works to understand the numbers in the display.

Do you understand the basic financial tools that help you determine your business health?

Budget. Imagine for a moment a pilot who did not track the progress of a flight to make sure he was following the flight plan he filed before takeoff. Would the plane full of passengers reach the correct destination? And if it did, would it arrive on time?

A budget is a businesses flight plan. It provides the means for you to determine what your projected revenue will be for the year, and to estimate what you think you will need to spend to hit that target. A budget also shows how much profit you expect to put in your pocket or invest further into the business. Without a budget, you have no flight plan—a very risky proposition for even the most experienced pilots. And like other vital statistics, you should review your budget at least monthly; otherwise, your business may fly off course.

It doesn't matter whether a budget is simple or complex, so long as it includes all of the critical variables. Some businesses may need just ten or twenty line items in their budget; others may need hundreds. Nor does it matter who prepares the budget. Some business leaders do the prep work themselves, others rely on an accountant or financial advisor to handle the budget, leaving them free to focus on other aspects of the business.

There is no debate, however, about the fact that there needs to be a budget, and someone needs to track it regularly. How does your company score when it comes to budget?

History. Any business more than a few years old has a set of historical numbers that describe its performance over time. This is an important record for a number of reasons. For one thing, it keeps you from repeating your mistakes, and it makes it easier for you to duplicate your successes. A business history also gives you perspective and helps you to recognize the cadence and pace of your company.

To help understand what I mean by cadence and pace, imagine a veteran competitive runner preparing for a ten-kilometer race. She relies on the experience of past races for everything from pre-race workouts and diet to actual race tactics. The history of performance in previous races helps her determine what pace she can sustain and how much water to drink to maximize efficiency. Without this history, she will almost certainly not perform as well and may even be injured.

Your business history works in the same way. It helps you to know when to invest marketing dollars to realize the best returns, to understand optimal staff levels and hours of operation, and to determine how much growth your company can comfortably sustain.

History should not be followed blindly, however. Circumstances change, and what worked in the past may not work as well in the future. But a healthy business cannot ignore its history.

History is as real as it gets. It's not debatable, it's not subjective, and it doesn't care how you are feeling today. As businesses move to higher levels of fitness and health, they use historical data to drill into trends and complex ratios that are less obvious.

Score This Fitness Key

While all of these elements are interrelated, it is possible to perform better in some than in others. Review each element of this fitness key:

Vital numbers: Do you know your company's vital statistics?

Guided by numbers: Do you rely on vital statistics as a basis for action?

Regular review: How often do you review important business metrics?

Financial tools: Can you interpret a profit and loss statement and a balance sheet?

Budget: Does your company operate with a budget? Does someone monitor the budget regularly?

History: Do you use past performance to guide future plans?

Do you know your numbers? Rate your organization on a scale of 1 to 10. (Use decimals if needed.)

Knowing Your Numbers. Write in your score: _____

Systems and Processes

"It's a dream until you write it down, then it's a goal."

-Anonymous

Many years ago, I undertook a weight-loss program. The program was a system designed to move participants through a series of phases in a predetermined sequence, beginning with conditioning and deconstruction, progressing through reconstruction and implementing change, and finally ending with monitoring and strengthening. Each step in the process built on the steps that came before so that all of the changes I was making to my diet and exercise regimen were simultaneously advanced and reinforced at each phase. The result was that I lost about ten pounds in twenty-one days.

Prior to starting the program, I had the desire to lose weight, but I had no clear picture of how to go about it. The changes I had been making to my diet and exercise routine were a haphazard and uncoordinated combination of tips and advice from magazine articles or conversations with friends. In my enthusiasm to try everything, I accomplished nothing.

The successful weight-loss program was different in a number of critical ways. The method it prescribed had worked for thousands of other people under circumstances similar to mine. The phased sequence gave me the structure I needed to make the necessary changes, and the monitoring component helped me measure results. Plus, the step-by-step character of the system made it easier to change my routine, and helped my new diet and exercise regimen to become routine.

Great businesses create and use systems in the same way and for the same reasons. Business systems standardize responses to routine situations and incorporate proven solutions to common problems. They increase efficiency and ensure that the means to achieving any desired outcome are available to everyone in the company. People change, business objectives change, but systems and processes remain steady.

Write it down. I believe you need to create systems in a particular way, and that begins with written plans and records. This is not just my opinion; it comes from many interviews with successful businesspeople. When I asked them what they would recommend to help other business owners become more successful, the one answer that everyone could agree on was that people need to write things down. This may sound obvious, but an experience I had a number of years ago taught me not to take it for granted. I asked a group of business owners who sold different types of remodeling and construction services to write down their sales process. It seemed like an easy task given that they or their staff were involved in some kind of sales activity many times each day. I was surprised to find, however, that most of them really struggled with the exercise and, although the services they all sold were very similar, the number of steps in the sales processes the group described varied from three to fourteen.

Are any of your key business processes—marketing, sales, production, and so on—written down? The act of recording these processes in writing makes it easier for you to evaluate them, and makes it possible for you to compare them to the processes of others in your field. Written systems and processes also make it easier to communicate them properly and to train others to master them.

You don't need an MBA or a business consultant to have written systems and processes. You can begin with a simple handwritten outline that captures the most critical steps. As the business grows and moves to a higher level of effectiveness, you will want to increase the amount of detail and also reach outside your own experience for new perspectives. But it all begins with identifying your business's three to five key processes and simply writing down the five to ten most critical steps in each process.

Functions, not personalities. It is also important to avoid creating systems and processes that depend on individual personalities. This is a trap that many small business owners fall into. Because they founded the business, most of the in-place systems and processes reflect their personal preferences. Worse, because many of them were new to the business, they made many mistakes and suffered through many false starts, all of which may now be preserved in the company's systems and processes.

People are the greatest asset of most businesses, but people can also be a real liability if systems and processes have evolved around individual personalities. Unfortunately, there are many false clues about the importance of individuals in popular culture. In sports, for example, it often appears that teams rely on individual players for their success. This impression is reinforced by the television coverage; cameras and commentators are focused on the most spectacular plays by individual players. But most successful professional sports teams are grounded in fundamentals that are not part of the weekly highlight reel. Their game plans leverage the strengths of individuals, but they are ultimately based on processes and systems that operate on and off the field.

To determine whether your systems are based on individual personalities, ask yourself if there are different standards for different individuals. Are your company's top performers called to the mat when they violate a system or process, or do they get special treatment? And what about the leaders in your company? Do they follow the rules the same as anybody else?

Communication. Good systems will fail without good communication. Another benefit to written systems is the protection they provide against miscommunication. We have all played the game where one person whispers something to the person next to them, who passes it on to the next person, and so on. By the time the last person passes it back to the originator, the message bears no resemblance to what it was when it began. On the other hand, pass a written message around the same table and there may be differences of interpretation, but everyone gets the same message.

Systems and communication grow in importance as a business grows. Again, small businesses often suffer from having been started by an individual who kept track of everything. The system is obvious to him because he invented it and has been using it for years. But as soon as a company adds a few team members, the system must now work for everyone. Clear communication becomes essential.

Communication vehicles include everything from annual meetings to e-mail blasts to automated voicemails and newsletters to one-on-one updates and coaching. What works best will depend on the type of information being communicated and the context in which it is received. If your businesses philosophy is "open book," then you will need to find ways to effectively communicate financial metrics to people who don't know anything about profit and loss statements.

Team surveys can help you figure out what information is sticking and how the team feels about the level of communication. If you are exhausted by the effort required for good business communication, you are not alone. Larger companies often hire communications directors to focus on both external and internal communications.

Training. Systems and processes are perpetuated through formal training. Imagine a runner who does not train for a race, or a tennis player who does not practice before a match, or a golfer who just walks onto the course without hitting the driving range or putting green. Unthinkable, but that is what we do in business every day.

Years ago I heard a successful person in the restaurant business say in a speech that training is an investment, not an expense. I think the distinction is very important. Training is often at the top of the list of cuts when businesses look for places to trim expenses. But if people are a business's greatest asset, then training is an essential investment in their care and feeding. Training teaches something new, gets rid of bad habits, conditions for additional strength, and is essential to growth. Training can be about immediate education—your company's product or service, or its systems and processes—or it can address more personal skills, such as time management. In all cases, training not only improves performance and efficiency, it helps you to retain the best people in your organization. You will also see improvement in attitude and commitment. We are in an age when employees are seeking more than just a job or a paycheck; they are looking for opportunity. In the remodeling business, it used to be that carpenters would jump from one company to the next for fifty cents more per hour. Today, people in these positions are asking about career paths and opportunities.

In business, training is a growth strategy, and a lack of commitment to it will result not only in poor results but also in poor overall health. One way to evaluate and quantify the training component of this fitness element is to ask yourself how many hours per week or month are dedicated to a team member's improvement. In my organization, between one and two weeks per year of each team member's time is devoted to improvement.

Evaluate performance. Just as we are conducting a fitness check on your business, your individual team members need the same check on their own fitness. Without a performance evaluation process, it is difficult to judge how well you are communicating, how effective training is, and how other relevant systems are working.

Performance evaluation is like a visit to the doctor. A doctor begins by measuring specific benchmarks, like weight, blood pressure, and heart rate, then uses the results to compare against past results. In addition to these objective measures, the doctor will generally spend a little time asking about what has changed in your life, how you have been feeling, and what, if anything, has been bothering you. These questions allow him or her to combine subjective data with the objective measures to make a recommendation, which typically includes changes in behavior as well as a time for a follow-up appointment.

Similarly, a performance evaluation is a one-on-one process that begins with taking inventory, moves to open discussion of what's working and what's not, examines short- and long-term goals, and, finally, develops a game plan for success. The evaluation process needs to occur regularly—at least once a year—and it needs to be consistent.

Score This Fitness Key

All businesses have systems and processes, but are yours effective? How do team members feel about them? Are they in sync with your company's size and growth trajectory? Are they impartial and are they consistent?

Review each element of this fitness key:

Write it down: Are your key business processes recorded, step-by-step, in writing?

Functions, not personalities: Do the same standards apply to everyone? Do top performers get special treatment?

Communication: Do you have an internal communication system that works? How do you know?

Training: How many hours per month are devoted to formal training?

Evaluate performance: Do you conduct evaluations on everyone at least once each year?

Are your systems and processes working? Rate your organization on a scale of 1 to 10. (Use decimals if needed.)

Systems and Processes. Write in your score: _____

Leadership

"Success demands singleness of purpose."
- Vince Lombardi

Everyone can recognize strong leadership when they see it, but it's difficult to evaluate leadership within your own organization without first understanding some of the individual characteristics that define it. Like many of the criteria for a healthy business, leadership has characteristics that may seem at odds with each other. For example, leaders should be strong, but also empathetic; they should excel at motivating and communicating to a large audience, but they must also be effective in one-on-one interactions.

Reflect on the following six elements of leadership, then score your business on its leaders and leadership characteristics.

Purpose. Strong leaders have a clear sense of purpose. Often, this purpose is the core feature of a company's mission statement, and it may take the form of a tagline, motto, or theme. A strong leader ensures that the company's purpose is understood by everyone at all levels within the organization by making it the centerpiece of all business communications and interactions, and by incorporating it into all business decisions. Although a company's sense of purpose is vulnerable during times of rapid growth, strong leaders work hard to ensure that no one loses sight of it.

Can you state clearly and concisely the purpose of your organization or company? If you asked five team members that question, would you get the same answer? Do you feel your company leaders have articulated the one or two key concepts that enable all employees to act in unison? Can you name the themes that control your business decisions? Are these rallying cries articulated frequently and reinforced at every opportunity?

Vision. A business leader needs a strong vision of where the company is heading. Everyone has vision to some degree, but the vision of company leaders operates on many different levels. To understand what I mean, think about the "vision" of craftsmen or production line team members. They are focused on what they need to accomplish today or perhaps by the end of the week. They are typically concerned only with their own immediate needs and those of the team of which they are a part, and they give their attention only to the one or two projects with which they are currently involved.

A manager's vision is more complex. Managers share the same narrowly focused vision, but they also need to look further ahead in time to goals for the month or the quarter. And a manager's vision is concerned with many individuals or several teams, as well as with multiple projects.

The vision of company leaders is even more complex. They need to look beyond the daily, weekly, monthly, and quarterly goals to see where the company is headed several years into the future. And their vision must encompass all projects and all team members.

Think about these skills as a set of camera lenses. A good leader needs to be able to focus clearly not only in the one-foot range, but also at the one-hundred-foot range. He or she needs to be able to zoom in, but also to change quickly to a wide-angle view. In some leaders, this ability is innate, in others it is learned; but in all cases it is essential. Does your company leadership have a strong vision?

Communication. This is where most companies meet their greatest challenges. Effective communication begins with deciding what gets communicated and what does not. More information isn't necessarily better, and a little information in the hands of the right person can go a long way.

Leaders care not only about what gets communicated but also how it is communicated. In today's business environment, communication needs to be both "high tech" and "high touch." E-mail may work well for communicating a list of materials to a group, but a phone call works better if more than a little discussion is required. And a face-to-face meeting works best when the message needs to carry energy or emotion. A good leader knows when each type of communication is appropriate.

Planning. A strong leader not only knows where the organization is heading, he or she creates a blueprint for how it will get there. A good plan also takes into account the resources needed to execute it. As obvious as this may seem, most small- to mid-size businesses have no written business plan. This has advantages—it enables them to take whatever comes their way—but also disadvantages—they constantly find themselves in circumstances not of their choosing and for which they are unprepared.

Lack of a written plan is management by accident. It is like shopping for dinner ingredients without a grocery list and not knowing how much money is in your wallet. As you wander aimlessly from aisle to aisle, you fill your cart with whatever items strike your fancy. When you reach the checkout counter, you discover you have too much of this and not enough of that. And because the total cost is more than you have to spend, you need to quickly decide what to give up. If you shop this way you will not go hungry, but you may not like what you end up having to eat. If you manage this way, you will not like the results any better.

A plan does not have to be inflexible or foolproof. In fact, strong leaders need to be creative, and should include alternatives and allow for contingencies. But they must also understand the difference between a free-wheeling brainstorming discussion and a planning session that results in action steps and clear levels of accountability.

There is an old saying: "If you fail to plan, plan to fail." I am also fond of saying, "Plan your work today, every day, then work your plan." Do you feel there is a strong playbook in your company, or is the leadership just winging it?

Empathy. Empathy is a mix of compassion, understanding, and sympathy, and in the hands of good leadership, empathy becomes contagious within organizations. Empathy is why people stay with organizations. It is the fuel that gets everyone through the inevitable tough times.

You can't see or touch empathy, but it is easy to recognize. A leader's empathy must be diverse and inclusive. It must extend to the team members with the lowliest tasks as well as to people at the highest levels of the company and to other leaders. Empathy extends also to clients, where it enables a deeper understanding of the anxieties that affect their decision-making processes. And empathy extends to suppliers, trade contractors, strategic partners, and all other business relationships as well.

Are your leaders empathetic? Is your company culture one of understanding, sympathy, and compassion?

Respect. Respect is what people say about you. Respect begins with one's own employees and co-workers, and it's often easy to evaluate a leader's performance simply by listening to what people are saying in idle conversations around the coffee machine. Strong leaders win respect not only within their company but outside as well, from other business leaders and from the community at large. Respect takes a long time to attain, but it can be lost very quickly.

Is your leadership well respected by the team, by your competition, and in your community?

Score This Fitness Key

Strong leaders make for healthy businesses. Owners find themselves in positions of leadership by default, and often have to work to master the necessary skills. Review each element of leadership:

Purpose: Can you name your company's main purpose? Would most team members come up with the same answer?

Vision: Do your leaders have both short- and long-term vision?

Communication: Does your company communicate enough of the right information to the right people in an effective way?

Planning: Are your leaders guided by a plan, or are they making it up as they go along?

Empathy: Is your company culture one of understanding, sympathy, and compassion toward team members, clients, vendors, and other business partners?

Respect: Are your leaders well respected, inside and outside your company?

Based on the above elements, rate the overall level of leadership within your organization on a scale of 1 to 10. (Use decimals if needed.)

Leadership. Write in your score: _____

Team

"Nothing can stop the man with the right mental attitude from achieving his goal; nothing on earth can help the man with the wrong attitude."
-Thomas Jefferson

Often when I am speaking to a business audience, I ask people to raise their hands if they feel like they have a great team. It's no surprise that almost every hand in the room goes up. Everybody believes they know what makes for a fit and healthy team, and everybody rates their own team quite highly before they go through our little fitness checkup. But after they drill down into all of the elements of a team, they usually come to see that while they have good people and enjoy working with them, they have a long way to go before they can really call themselves a *team*.

High retention. Most businesses on a path to growth and constant improvement need a core group of individuals who stay with the company year after year. This kind of retention of long-term employees, although difficult to achieve, is easy to evaluate. If your business appears to be a revolving door or you are constantly hiring with minimal growth, then your retention score will be low. High retention is an indicator of business health.

When a business truly values people as its greatest asset, it gains not only a feel-good theme song but also a smart

63

economic strategy. Most businesses can quantify the level of investment that a team member represents. In some businesses it may be as little as ten to twenty thousand dollars per individual, but often it is many times that figure. Imagine the consequences if other investments in your portfolio suddenly vaporized. You would be firing your investment manager or stockbroker. Healthy businesses understand that the investment in the team is huge and make retention a priority. They communicate this in a variety of ways, from highlighting individual anniversary dates at staff meetings to establishing an annual award for "lifetime achievement" or "continuing service."

Top performers. I think when it comes to the concept of a team, professional sports are a great model for business. A professional sports team can have a good game or a winning season for a variety of reasons. They can win because of a positive attitude or because they have a great game plan. Occasionally, they can win because of a fluke or a timely error by the opponent. But it's certain that they cannot win year after year without strong individual performers. It's wonderful to have a group of average folks working together in love and harmony; but to be successful year after year and take a business to high levels of performance, you need some players who make the all-star team. These high-performing individuals raise the bar for everyone on the team. These people may not necessarily move to higher levels within the organization, but they address their role and their world with mastery.

Whether top performers come from within your company or from the outside, they are an important part of a healthy business. Top performers are creative and make suggestions for new ways to improve and differentiate. Top performers are emulated by others and become additional mentors for your team. As you reflect on your business's health, ask yourself if 10 percent or more of your team members meet these criteria. If so, then that is a positive sign.

Gung ho attitude. When hiring team members, you must ask three questions: Can they do the job? Will they do the job? Will they fit? Two of these three questions are not about competency. They are about attitude and culture. In today's business environment you cannot underestimate the importance of a team's attitude when determining health. A gung ho attitude can be the reason a customer comes back again. To continue the sports analogy, a gung ho attitude contributes the extra one percent that adds the winning point to the score.

In some businesses, it is easier to see the lack of this spirit than its presence. If the most common word you hear from team members is "No" or "That's not my job," then you have team members with an attitude problem. On the other hand, if your team does whatever it takes to delight the client without complaining about the extra effort, you have created a gung ho attitude.

Constant improvement. While many books, seminars, and other sources of business advice can inspire improvement, a true commitment to constant improvement comes from within the individual team members. When individuals wake up and realize that they are in control of their destinies and make a commitment to take ownership of their own improvement, an organization moves into high gear. Over the years I have worked with and taught thousands of businesspeople, and in the companies that have grown and become very successful, all of the team members have this common denominator. Many of the individuals who have excelled have attended less prestigious schools or had lower grades or just average scores on standard tests, but their drive to constantly learn and improve has lifted them above the crowd.

A healthy business not only recognizes this dynamic but also creates an environment to encourage the process. A fit business highlights team members who have improved, and they in turn become catalysts for more improvement and spur others to embrace this thinking. For the successful team, constant improvement becomes a habit; for the ultra-successful, it is an addiction.

Do the above describe many of your team members? Or have these kinds of individuals left your company and become your competitors?

Future leaders. Many years ago I asked a successful businessperson who had accomplished more than most in his twenty-year business career what the next step for him would be in his business. He said, "I am looking for someone to fire me."

I was taken aback at first by his answer, but as I thought about it I realized how important this attitude was to a healthy business. Most people find the notion of being fired disconcerting. But in most good businesses, the leaders have moved through passages that have been positive for the business but have helped them to grow personally as well. Think about the prospect of doing exactly what you are doing today in two to three years. It's not a comforting thought. Businesses need to position themselves for the future. Leaders need to be pushed forward by the force of the talent behind them.

By communicating the importance of future leaders, you instill the hope in strong individuals that there will be a place for them at a high level. This preparation not only involves thinking a few years out, but also an investment on the owner's part to mentor and coach the future leaders. Can you name the person or people that will replace you or the leadership in your business?

Growth oriented. Does your team want to grow with your business? Individual team members think about growth differently. Some are very growth oriented and see your business merely as a stepping stone to the "real job" on which they have set their sights. Others enjoy what they are doing and find it hard to imagine a future without you or the business. The real question comes down to this: do your team members see what they are doing as a job or as an opportunity?

A business with a truly high fitness score on "team" needs to believe that its growth will only occur if it is committed to team growth. When evaluating this business fitness criterion, think of as many examples as you can where individuals have grown as your business has grown. Do your team members see themselves in new roles at your business in the future? Are these issues that managers or leaders regularly discuss with team members?

Your company should have a plan for putting future leaders in place. There are many examples of how to go about this in other organizations. Many volunteer organizations or associations use a "leadership ladder" that creates a series of positions that serve as stepping-stones. While on the lower steps, individuals learn the ropes and gain valuable experience; assuming they perform well, they automatically ascend to the next level when their turn comes. Other organizations create a "buddy system" that pairs older, more experienced individuals with younger, less experienced individuals. This not only ensures the orderly, consistent transfer of corporate knowledge, it also provides an opportunity to identify team members that display an aptitude for leadership.

The process of planning for future leaders should be a priority and should not be kept a secret. It will make the great ones push harder than ever.

Exceed expectations. You can look at the word *expectation* in different ways. It could refer to budget predictions or it could refer to performance against quality standards. It could involve the amount of time involved in an activity or it could be as simple as delivering the product or service as promised.

Meeting expectations is a given for any business; exceeding expectations is necessary for growth and improvement. If you are ahead of budget, you make more money. If your team beats the schedule, then they are available to please other clients. I get many letters from clients about how a team member did something special, like helping a client shovel snow or find a lost dog. If the team does something unexpected like this for a client, it creates raving fans and a lot of referrals.

Exceeding expectations can occur anywhere in your company. It may be delivery of a project a few days early, or coming in below budget on the purchase of business equipment; or it could be anticipating a client concern or objection and having the solution already prepared. There is a fine line between exceeding and falling short, but one leads to success and the other to failure.

Exceeding expectations is a team culture issue that can really define a business as a team sport. Does your team exceed expectations, or do you find yourself and your clients disappointed? Does it seem as if you and your team are constantly putting out fires?

Accountability. Is there accountability at all levels? Accountability is an important indicator of general business fitness but specifically of team health. Accountability taps deeply into the belief system that failure is not an option.

In the remodeling business, like in many other businesses, some people sell and develop the business while others produce and build the projects. After monthly or quarterly projections are communicated properly, everyone needs to understand everything for which they are accountable. Having a playbook is meaningless unless it is executed. If the sales team is charged with signing one hundred thousand dollars in contracts each month, then they need to understand that not hitting these targets will affect the production flow. They need to appreciate that falling short could result in lost hours by production team members, and they need to understand the pain that loss of income will cause those families. This level of accountability translates into working weekends if it is required to hit the targets, or doing whatever else is required to meet these goals.

The flipside is also true. Remodeling production teams have different but equally important targets for which they are accountable. They need to meet deadlines to ensure crews are available for projects in the pipeline, and they need to stay within budgets to help meet economic goals. Like other team related elements, accountability has two sides. One is black and white, spelled out in the rulebook; the other is a gray area, an unwritten company cultural issue that is understood and lived by all.

Score This Fitness Key

As you evaluate your team's level of accountability, it is important to reflect at both levels. If the rulebook is fuzzy, then it may be a systems issue that needs addressing. If the rulebook is black and white and communicated properly, then the spotlight of accountability should shine on the team that is expected to deliver.

Review the elements of this fitness key:

Retention: Do you have many long-term employees?

Top performers: Does your team include some all-stars?

Gung ho attitude: Do people do whatever it takes?

Constant improvement: Is improvement second nature?

Future leaders: Have you identified and trained future company leaders?

Growth-oriented: Do you provide an environment that nurtures growth?

Exceeding expectations: Does your team go above and beyond the norm?

Accountability: Does everyone understand their responsibilities and take them seriously?

Do you have a great team? Rate your organization on a scale of 1 to 10. (Use decimals if needed.)

Team. Write in your score: _____

Product or Service

*"Quality in a service or product is not what you put into
it. It is what the client or customer gets out of it."*
- Peter Drucker

Often we confuse the quality of the product or service our business delivers with the health or fitness of the business itself. Most people believe that if a company delivers a good product or service, then the business must be in good shape. Although the two are certainly related, you cannot judge the book by the cover when it comes to basic business health.

Examples are not difficult to come by. Think about the number of times you have gone to a restaurant with great food for a fair price, then returned six or twelve months later to find the restaurant is out of business. Or maybe you have had an experience with a particular auto mechanic or other service technician who did great work, but complained openly about the company or business that he worked for. These are signs of a disconnect between a business and its end product. Let's begin our fitness analysis by looking at some of the less obvious indicators of health in this area.

Sweet spot. Let me finish a story I hinted at earlier. Many years ago while addressing a group of remodeling contractors, I asked them to tell me what the right-sized project was for their business. A fellow in the front row raised his hand and said "Anywhere from five to five hundred thousand dollars." A couple of more hands went up with answers like, "The bigger the better," or "I can handle jobs of any size." Then from the back of the room came the voice of my good friend, Jim Strite, a veteran contractor who is quite successful. He said, "Our ideal project is $72,500." It took a minute, but eventually the realization sank in to the other remodelers in the room that this was the kind of answer I had been looking for. Jim believes, as do I, that every business has a sweet spot. He knew precisely what his company was capable of and that was the work he went after. Most of the others in the room took whatever came along, the bigger the better, as they would say. Their "right-sized" project was simply whatever they happened to be working on at the moment. A business that succeeds by focusing on $72,500 projects has different processes and systems and staff than one that specializes in five thousand dollar projects or five hundred thousand dollar projects.

The better you can define your sweet spot, and the closer you can stay to it, the better you will perform. We see clear examples of this in a baseball team's pitching staff. If every baseball pitcher can throw strikes, then why do baseball teams maintain starters and mid-relievers and closers? It's because they have figured out the skills and limit of each pitcher's performance in terms of how many pitches they can throw effectively—the sweet spot—and they know that the way to win is to stay within those limits.

Many businesses focus on developing the core competence of the craft and ignore any consideration of what the ideal size for the business might be. You will see this in food service businesses. Some handle a dinner for four perfectly, but when you come back for a party with twenty, they fumble with the flow and communication. Knowing your ideal size gives you confidence to say "yes" when the right opportunity comes along, and, more importantly, it gives you a reason to say "no," regardless of how attractive the opportunity seems to be. If a current commitment takes you outside of your sweet spot, you will most likely miss out on other, more appropriate opportunities.

Ideal client. The same is true of knowing the right client for your business. Businesses that have a one-size-fits-all approach have a tough time with this, but high-end retailers understand this notion very well. Instead of casting a wide net hoping to catch everyone who walks in, high-end retailers understand that their merchandise and their pricing is going to turn most people away. They are not interested in doing business with people looking for a bargain; they train their staff to recognize someone searching for value. Everything in the store, from the window displays to the lighting to the style of the furniture, is carefully crafted to make the value shopper feel right at home. The sales staff is trained on where to stand, how long to wait before approaching, and what to say when they do speak with customers. The result is fewer clients who spend more and feel good about it.

As you reflect on this piece of the product-service puzzle, ask yourself if these crucial definitions are written down and are part of everyone's training. If they aren't, there is a good chance that your team members won't agree on what they are.

On-time delivery. Another way to judge a business's product or service fitness is whether or not they can deliver on time. How many times have you had a one p.m. appointment with the doctor or dentist, but had to wait for forty-five minutes to be seen? If this happens once in a while, you can overlook it, but if it happens regularly it's a sign that something is not right with the business. (Plenty of doctors who are excellent practitioners of medicine are mediocre businesspeople.) By contrast, when you order a light fixture from a distributor for a two-week delivery and it arrives in precisely fourteen days, it is a good sign that the business has its act together.

Every business faces the challenge of making sure the pace of delivery of its product or service is in sync with both the customer's expectation and also with other elements of the business. A good way to measure the health of your company with respect to on-time delivery is to sample client surveys or measure the amount of time staff devotes to making apologies to customers over missed schedules.

Quality of the advice. In business today, frontline staff need to know your product and service well, but they also must be able to act as consultants to help guide prospective clients through the maze of buying decisions. The staff needs to help the customer by asking the right questions, then leading him or her to the proper solution, even if it means recommending another product or service.

We see this with a good server in a restaurant who is asked to recommend an entree. If she rambles on and on about the meat dish and you are a vegetarian, then she has just wasted your time and her advice is useless. If, on the other hand, she first asks you a couple of simple questions like, "How hungry are you?" or "Do you have a preference toward seafood or meat?" then that dialog is much more likely to lead to good suggestions and a memorable dining experience.

There is, however, a balance between providing too much advice and too little. The customer or client probably approached your business initially with the intention of buying something, not to make a new friend or do a research project. High-quality advice can lead directly to a positive outcome; low-quality advice often results in a client who says, "Let me think about it," instead of making the purchase. Returns or exchanges of merchandise are other signs of poor advice, as are clients who ask for lots of changes mid-stream or after the fact.

Craftsmanship. Quality advice and a well-crafted product or service should go hand in hand, but they need to be peeled apart in this fitness exercise. Product quality is relative to client expectation. A restaurant customer may feel great about the decision to order the steak but will be disappointed if it is overcooked or too small. Similarly, if you go to a fast food restaurant, you know not to expect a fine dining meal. The reverse is also true: in a fine restaurant you do not expect your meal to be wrapped in paper.

Another quality indicator is what people are saying about your company. If you mostly hear that you are a little pricey but provide a great service, then that means your company is perceived as a good value. If, on the other hand, talk about craft is conspicuously absent from the conversation and people talk only about your price or compliment your team on their pleasant manner, then product quality may not be what it needs to be.

Flexibility. Does your product or service respond to diverse economic conditions? Important as it is to know the right size and client for your business, it is also necessary to be responsive to diverse economic conditions. In times like these, businesses need to differentiate themselves while also casting a wide enough net to capture a wide audience. In some cases, you may need to review the fundamental business model so as to make the numbers work.

The transformation of the movie theater is a good example of how one business responded to a changing market. As the expenses of making movies have skyrocketed, the cost to a theater to play first-run movies has also increased. Moreover, movie theaters compete with video stores and cable and satellite TV companies for viewers. Successful theaters locate in high foot-traffic areas, like malls, or close to public transportation hubs and thriving shops. They develop strategic alliances with nearby restaurants to ensure that "theatre menus" are available, and they set their prices at an accessible level.

The handyman business is another example of a product that responds well to diverse economic conditions. An established remodeling firm focuses primarily on medium- or larger-sized projects, and the staff, processes, and systems are all geared for that type of work and those kinds of clients. But when housing prices soften or interest rates rise, homeowners are less inclined to dive into a large remodeling project. As a result, many remodeling firms have diversified into the professional handyman business to complement their core remodeling business. This innovation helps these companies take the valley out of a dip in the market and provides for more sustainable growth.

Are you results predictable? The final gauge of product or service fitness is predictability. Imagine a restaurant owner who predicts that one hundred people will come in to eat on a Thursday night. If ninety-seven show up, we would all say that is a good sign that the owner understands who his customers are and what they want. On the other hand, if the business is designed and staffed for one hundred meals and only twenty-five customers show up, that would not be a good night, and is a sign that something is missing.

We have already discussed the importance of having a business plan and knowing your key numbers. A great way to judge the health of a business is to determine if your product or service is delivered as you predicted it would be. A healthy business is predictable.

Score This Fitness Key

As you think about your product or service, think about the business behind it. If, based on the above criteria, you feel your product or service is strong, then score it high; if reading this chapter has made you unsure and raised some questions, then be more conservative with your scoring.

Review each element of the fitness key:

Sweet spot: Do you know the optimum size and scope of your product or service?

Ideal client: Do you know what your best customers look like?

On-time delivery: Do you keep to your schedule consistently?

Advice: Are you a consultant to your clients or just another vendor?

Quality: Is your craftsmanship at a high enough level?

Flexibility: Can your product or service respond to changing markets?

Predictable results: Are you performing as you expected you would?

Does your product or service deliver? Rate your organization on a scale of 1 to 10. (Use decimals if needed.)

Product or Service. Write in your score: _____

Profitability

"The secret to winning is constant consistent management"
- Tom Landry

The way businesspeople think about and understand profitability varies greatly. At one end of the spectrum are those for whom making a profit is the primary motive for starting a business, and it is the ultimate goal or outcome of staying in business. For them, profitability is the score-card by which any business is measured. At the other end of the spectrum are those for whom the personal, social, or moral motivations for running a business take precedence. For them, profitability is part of a game they must master to satisfy tax regulations and accounting rules.

The views of most business owners, of course, are not so black and white. But no matter how you think about profitability, there is no denying that it is a critical element in determining business health. Even though there may be no right way to look at profitability, there is also no way to ignore it. To help determine your business fitness with regard to profitability, work through the following concepts. It is not uncommon to find that a business may fall short in some areas but score high in others.

Defining profit. It is surprising how many people do not understand basic concepts like gross profit and net profit. Many small-business owners operate out of a checkbook, so they tend to equate financial health with the size of their bank account at the moment in time when they check the balance. Obviously, they understand that the price of their product or service and the amount of business they do has a direct bearing on whether or not they have enough money to pay the bills every month, but that's where their knowledge (and often their interest) ends. In many instances, they find out whether their business operated at a profit or loss only once a year when they file their tax returns.

So the first fitness test for profitability is to answer one basic question: do you know what your profit is? At a minimum, a business owner ought to know whether or not the business is producing a net profit. The healthier the business, the more aware the owner is of gross margins, not only for his or her own company but for typical companies engaged in the same business. Even better is to understand gross and net margins for each of the specific products or services your business provides, and how those margins fluctuate seasonally.

Your team should also understand these concepts, and they should be able to name at least a few of the elements—like overhead, inventory, labor, and so on—that influence profitability. If you or your team think that what you have just read sounds like a foreign language, then you may have plenty of room to improve your understanding of profitability.

Predictability. If you were to ask a serious runner how he thinks he will perform in a race, he would probably be able to predict a targeted time as well as where he would place in the competition. More than good guesses, predictions like this are reasonable estimates based on a history of past performance. And the ability to achieve predicted results is a sign of a runner's fitness.

Similarly, in a healthy business, results are predictable. In fact, as I have grown business units in our company as well as studied other businesses, I have found that the ability to predict profit accurately is more critical to business health than achieving the highest profit. For example, a healthy business should be able to predict how many customers it will serve this month, what their average spend will be and, therefore, what profit will be. If actual profit is one thousand dollars instead of five thousand, then something is obviously wrong. The business may be improperly staffed, may not be offering the right product mix, or may have too many returns. On the flipside, if profit is double what was predicted, that windfall could be a sign of serious problems on the horizon. It might mean that the business is now out of inventory and will be unable to adequately serve future customers. The high profits could also be a sign of too few staff members or staff that are not adequately compensated to ensure retention.

Are your profits as you predicted them to be? If your profitability is within five percent of your predictions, then your business should score high on this portion of the checkup. But if actual profitability varies by a larger amount, then it is a sign that this aspect of your business's fitness could do with further testing and examination.

Improvement. A good indication of a healthy profitability score is consistent improvement. A business that is committed to providing future opportunities for team members will work to ensure that profits trend upward. The magnitude of the increase is less important; for that matter, so is the need for an increase every year. In fact, straight-line improvement is more the exception than the rule, and most businesses will experience occasional hiccups and small fluctuations. However, a healthy business will be able to withstand a short-term downtick, and will recover more quickly.

What profitability trend do you see with your company? Go back five or ten years and track year-over-year changes to margins and net profits. If the trend is downward, ask why. If it is because you decided to invest heavily by making additional hires or purchasing new equipment or technology, then you have less reason for concern. But if it is because you misjudged the market, your sales targets were off, or productivity fell, it may indicate a need for reassessment.

Balance. We frequently hear about "balanced diets" or "work-life balance" regarding our physical health—perhaps because it is easy for us to overshoot in one direction or the other. Vegetables are good for us, but we have to make sure that we also eat other kinds of foods; a strong work ethic is important to business success, but not if it adversely affects our relationship with our spouse or children.

Similarly, profit balance is an indictor of business health. This is not a question of predicting profit levels or rates of improvement; rather, it is a question of what the business does with its profits. A start-up company may use its profits to satisfy short-term needs, such as improving wages or acquiring essential technology to boost productivity or to increase marketing to capture more business. A more mature company may set aside capital for future acquisitions or invest in longer-term programs, such as employee benefit plans.

As you reflect on your business, think about whether essential technologies will be up-to-date in three to five years. Ask yourself if your processes and systems are adequate to meet the needs of a changing market place. Are you investing in future leaders? Is your physical plant adequate to accommodate growth? The answers to questions like these will help you evaluate whether your profitability is being applied in a balanced way.

Score This Fitness Key

The ability to achieve profits that are predictable and stable is critical to business health. How profits are spent varies at different stages of development, but a balance between short- and long-term goals is essential. Review each element of this fitness key:

Defining profit: Do you know what your profit is?

Predictability: Are profits within five percent of what you budgeted?

Improvement: Are profits stable or trending upward?

Balance: Do you invest profits in both short- and long-term goals?

Is your business profitable? Rate your organization on a scale of 1 to 10. (Use decimals if needed.)

Profitability. Write in your score: _____

Reputation

"What you get by achieving your goals is not as important
as what you become by achieving your goals"
- Zig Ziglar

As with our personal health and fitness, some business fitness criteria are obvious through casual observation while others
require sophisticated testing and examination. Reputation
is just such an element. It has internal and external aspects
and becomes more and more important as business leaders
mature in their careers. Like the other fitness keys, we will look
at reputation from different points of view to help you be more
objective when scoring this part of the checkup.

Respect. Is your business respected in your industry and
marketplace? Remember, being respected is not the same as being
well liked. While respect may stem from your charitable efforts or from
your activism in the community or the industry, it may arise just as easily
among competitors that lose business to your company, or from the size of
your market share.

Respect may also come through the interest local or national media
show in your company. Although media attention comes naturally to business owners who are outgoing and always looking for a podium, it can
also be achieved by those who are quiet and modest—those who like to

fly under the radar. Obviously, the media attention I'm referring to has no relation to sensationalized stories that paint a negative picture of your industry. If you're showing up in those, that most certainly is a sign of poor business health (and maybe some much bigger problems). But it is a sign of business health if you appear in local stories highlighting your business accomplishments or your involvement in community activities. Mention in regional and national stories is even better.

Referrals. Every customer who refers a friend or relative to your business is a sign of respect. This may sound obvious, but a surprising number of businesses don't know what their referral rate is. If you're unsure of this fundamental metric, it's a sign that there is room for improvement. If you track your referrals and they are above 90 percent, that is a good indicator of business fitness; if they are below 50 percent, it is not healthy.

Marketing budget. One way to gauge the strength of your reputation is to compare your marketing costs to those of competitors or industry averages. A good reputation is usually a magnet for new clients, and if clients are seeking you out, marketing costs go down. On the flipside, high marketing costs means you have to work hard to generate customers, and that could be a sign of a poor reputation. And if your marketing costs are changing, your reputation may also be changing, for better or worse.

Close rates. Are you closing sales or converting prospects into paying clients at a rate that is above or below industry averages? A high close rate is a good indicator of a good reputation. Although a low close rate is often rationalized as the effect of a slumping market, high prices, or poor lead qualification, it could tell you something about your reputation. Before you jump on your salespeople, do a little investigating into how the company is perceived; a tarnished reputation may not be the main reason sales are off, but it could be an important piece of the puzzle.

Recruiting. Does your business attract talent? If you ask a group of young Little Leaguers which three major league baseball teams they would like to play for, the "home" team will often be at the top of their list, but the other two will probably be the teams that squared off in last year's World Series. Why? Because these teams have a reputation of being at the top; they get the media exposure, are consistently winners, and they attract the best talent.

There is a strong parallel in business. A company with a great reputation is a magnet for talent; a company with a weak reputation will be left with the dregs. It's not hard to tell which is which. Look at the response when you advertise for an open position; all things being equal, if you get a large number of qualified applicants, it is a sign of a good reputation. Also think about the strongest candidates for an open position: are they seeking out your company or are you chasing them down? How many times does an existing employee recommend a friend? These kinds of indicators should give you a good feel for your reputation as seen through the eyes of folks who are considering joining your team.

Raving fans. Creating "satisfied" customers isn't good enough any more. Today, a business needs "raving fans"—customers who sing the company's praises without being asked. These customers are committed to you, and the thought of using another firm makes them feel guilty. Raving fans look for ways to improve your business's success and are willing to participate beyond a vendor-client relationship. They see themselves as an integral part of your growth and will support you in a down market.

All businesses have some raving fans, but the question is how many? Can you name ten raving fans or is it a struggle to think of even a few? What percentage of your clients are raving fans? Is that number increasing week to week? Are your team members actively trying to cultivate that level of loyalty?

Legal problems. Businesses today must operate in a very litigious climate. Legal challenges can stem from a variety of causes—employment issues, client disputes, and regulatory challenges—so it is difficult to quantify the effect they have on a business's reputation. Keep in mind, however, that an abundance of legal challenges generally indicates a poorer reputation.

You might also be fortunate not to have stepped on a land mine. On the other hand, success makes you more of a target. If that's the case, check to see if the amount you are spending on legal fees is in sync with the times, your industry, your scale of business, or your growing pains. Consider also whether you are on the offensive or defensive side of the table.

Score This Fitness Key

As we have discussed, there are many ways to look at a reputation of a business. Whether you see reputation as a result of actions, team, or a product of evolution and culture, the importance of it remains. Your score for reputation will set a benchmark you can use for comparison when you come back for your annual checkup.

Review each element of this fitness key:

Respect: It's nice to be well liked, but is your company well respected?

Referrals: Do you get a lot of referrals? Do you know how many?

Marketing budget: How does your budget measure up to that of other companies?

Close rates: Are you selling a higher or lower percentage of prospects?

Recruiting: Do you attract high quality job applicants or are you chasing after talent?

Raving fans: Can you name ten customers who are raving fans?

Legal problems: Are you embroiled in legal battles?

What is your business's reputation? Rate your organization on a scale of 1 to 10. (Use decimals if needed.)

Reputation. Write in your score: _____

Stress

"A man who is too busy to take care of his health is like a mechanic that is too busy to take care of his tools."
- Spanish Proverb

In our personal lives, we know that stress affects our health. Modern medicine shows that stress can weaken our immune system, making us vulnerable to disease and exacerbating existing physical infirmities. These effects occur whether the stress is externally imposed or internally generated. In some cases, both the cause and the cure for stress are obvious, but frequently we need professional help to get relief. Regardless, it is generally clear to us whether we are handling stress well or not.

Businesses that experience unhealthy levels of stress can also suffer negative effects, while those that have stress levels under control generally thrive and grow. As we examine how stress affects your business fitness, keep an open mind and try to score this fitness key as objectively as possible.

Focus. It is impossible to touch and feel time, but one thing is certain: there is a fixed amount of it available each day. Some of the time you devote to business has to do with day-to-day concerns, whether it's purchasing raw materials, making a sale, doing the books, or tending to one of the hundreds of tasks that are essential to success. But businesspeople often fail to spend enough time taking in the big picture and reflecting what next month or next year might bring. The more fit the business, the more the owner's time is divided proportionately among the full range of activities. It may be impossible to determine an exact allocation of time for different levels of focus, but we know that a healthy business needs to dedicate some real time to working *on* the business and not just *in* the business trenches.

I've heard this called "non-productive" time because it is not directly related to the creation or delivery of any product or service, but this term is misleading. Time spent advancing the vision of a business is among the most productive an owner can spend. It may include time directed toward looking for ways to improve processes. Or it can be time spent coaching team members, not just on how to accomplish today's tasks, but also on how to prepare themselves for upcoming challenges. It might mean time spent developing new products or services, or simply evaluating the need for them.

An excellent way to distill these multiple levels of focus is to imagine looking at a mountain landscape. A nearsighted person might see a nearby flower clearly but not the leaves on trees one thousand feet away. A person with better vision can see the nearby flowers as well as be able to identify individual leaves on the trees but might not be able to make out a rock formation on the distant mountain. But a person with the ability to focus on short-, middle-, and long-range objects would see all of these things clearly. In the same way, when a business is in balance, attention is focused on short-, middle-, and long-term goals.

Proactive vs. reactive. Another indication of business stress is the degree to which circumstances control how time is spent. A reactive business lacks control of circumstances and responds to one crisis after another. A proactive business manipulates circumstances to avoid or minimize crises and thereby controls how resources are expended.

Being proactive means taking preemptive action. For example, getting yearly checkups is proactive and preventative, enabling people to catch symptoms of possible illness sooner and deal with the problem before it gets critical. Failing to visit the doctor on a regular basis, however, could allow serious illness to develop and lead to more expensive and prolonged treatment.

All businesses and business owners are both reactive and proactive, but the most successful devote a much higher percentage of energy and resources to proactive activities. Being proactive is not only more effective, but it also helps to mitigate stress for you, your team, and your clients. With less stress, processes work as designed, people are more accountable to each other, and everyone thinks more clearly and makes better decisions.

Depending on your business, you may be able to measure directly the proportion of proactive to reactive activity. Often the most telling factor is how you, as the business owner, spend your time. If you are constantly interrupted throughout the day by crises involving staff, customers, or vendors, then you may be stuck in a reactive mode. If, on the other hand, your day proceeds more or less as planned and crises are either averted or handled adeptly by others, then you are most likely operating in a proactive mode. Most business owners will find themselves somewhere between these extremes, but with a little attention you can easily determine if you are leaning one way or the other.

A rule of thumb is that successful businesspeople spend about 80 percent of their time proactively and 20 percent reactively. A good test for your team is to ask them to calculate their individual ratios. Even fit businesses will find a wide variation, but give yourself a healthier score on stress if you and your team are generally more proactive.

Effort. The amount of time you need to devote to the business is an indicator of stress fitness. If you and your team members are able to limit hours worked to forty-five to fifty-five per week, you are handling stress reasonably well. The key word in this question, though, is *able*. Some people are so passionate and fired up about the business that they leap out of bed in the morning and dive into the day's opportunities. Others have no choice but to invest sixty hours or more just to keep the business afloat.

Business longevity and maturity will also influence the amount of effort required. Most companies in the first few years of operation require more attention. Like the parents who must spend every waking hour—and many sleepless nights—tending to the needs of a newborn, the owner of a start-up business will need to spend many hours learning the business while also operating the business. As a business grows, however, more resources are available to hire staff and acquire timesaving technology, so the time requirement should diminish.

Regardless of the maturity of your business, however, one good indication of stress related to hours worked is to ask yourself if you are able to spend adequate time with your family and friends, or even with your own outside interests. If you are feeling guilty or frustrated about these relationships and activities, then the number of hours you are spending on the business may be out of balance.

Cadence. I spoke earlier about pace in connection with knowing your numbers. The pace of business also affects levels of stress. A business that runs at full throttle day after day creates intolerable levels of stress that will likely cause it to fail. Likewise, if the business cadence feels like a snail's pace, the business is unlikely to grow or improve and will also fail. As with so many other aspects of a fit business, determining a healthy pace is critical.

As I have already mentioned, work to establish a pace that is "aggressive but realistic." "Aggressive" means that on a scale of 1 to 10, you are at an 8; you are moving swiftly but you are not operating at full speed—there is something left in reserve should you need to "accelerate," like a car moving into the passing lane. A "realistic" pace provides balance and indicates that our goals will not require a heroic effort to be accomplished. Being realistic means we have a point of reference—most often past performance—that informs us of what is possible.

Score This Fitness Key

There is no question that stress is a byproduct of the business environment. But I think it is important to understand that stress is also a factor in its own right—one that can have dramatic influence on business fitness. Review each element of this fitness key:

Focus: Do you spend time working "on" the business, not just "in" the trenches?

Proactive vs. reactive: Do you control your time or are you always reacting to crises?

Effort: Are you and your staff working a reasonable numbers of hours?

Cadence: Does the business operate at an "aggressive but realistic" pace?

Rate your organization on a scale of 1 to 10. (Use decimals if needed.)

Stress. Write in your score: _____

Positioning

"If you don't know where you are going, you will wind up somewhere else."
- Yogi Berra

When it comes to our personal health and fitness, we know that the habits and investments we make now will pay dividends later when we need to draw from our fitness account. We work on short-term fixes immediately, but as we become healthier we become just as focused on the long-term results. The same is true in business—the effects of good positioning on your business fitness may not be apparent until some time in the future.

That said, a business could be so obsessed with future results that it loses touch with today. In a fit business, all pieces of the positioning puzzle should be in balance and harmony. Let's begin to break apart the concept of positioning.

Stable and consistent. Stability is the foundation for improvement. In a stable business, there are few surprises and a high level of predictability. When changes do occur, they are gradual and relatively minor. A stable business is one whose product and service delivery is under control.

A wonderful family restaurant in my town is a great example of what I mean by stability. Week after week, the same kitchen and wait staff serves the same group of patrons, and the result is a very consistent experience on both sides. With stability like this, the owner and head chef can experiment with minor changes to the menu or hours of operation or pricing with almost no risk. The consistency provides a background against which the business can introduce new features without disturbing its core offering.

This kind of positioning is like having a ladder that is so stable you can climb it with confidence. Because you are not worried about falling, you can reach a little higher and focus all of your attention on the task at hand. An unstable ladder has the opposite effect: it undermines your confidence, distracts your attention, and makes you less effective.

Strong market awareness. In today's fast-paced, high-risk business world every company needs keen insights into the changing needs of its customers. But local knowledge is no longer enough; business owners must be aware of the effect the larger economy or world events can have on their business. Market awareness also means being sensitive to the demographic and generational differences among both your team and your clients.

In business today, everyone has to keep up—they have to be in the wave of the strongest trends. But in a healthy business with strong market awareness, you can also see what is ahead and behind the wave. Knowing which indicators to watch is like shining a light on a dark and foggy environment. In the remodeling world, we keep an eye on consumer confidence ratings and home value appreciation. Interest rates have less of an effect unless there are big adjustments. In retailing, where money is made or lost during the holiday season, market awareness is important on a macro scale: predicting the latest video game or clothing craze can create lines of customers waiting for the store to open.

Market awareness is a useful tool to use to examine your day-to-day decisions. None of us has a crystal ball, and luck sometimes plays a role—but if you ask the right questions and look for insights and patterns, the opportunity to be lucky increases.

Well-capitalized. Many variables can cause the failure of a business, but one common denominator that pops up frequently is being under capitalized. This is surprising, considering that most people understand the concept in other aspects of their lives. For example, most people who are going on a long car trip would make sure they had fuel in the car's tank and a credit card to refill the tank along the way. There are secondary consequences, too. In addition to failing to reach your destination, starting without enough fuel or a means to purchase it might limit your ability to change your route along the way. A fifty-mile detour to take in an interesting local attraction might not be possible for fear of running low on gasoline.

Being well-capitalized allows a business to make decisions based on what is best rather than on the amount of money in the bank today. With capital, you can take advantage of buying opportunities, invest in marketing when you need to prime the pump, or recruit an all-star player who unexpectedly becomes available.

The goal of this part of your checkup is not to address good or bad sources of capital or even the amount of capital you should have. It is simply to ascertain whether you are capitalizing appropriately to position your business for the future.

Diversified for risk. Many years ago, investors were limited to investing in individual stocks. The stocks might have fallen in different sectors, but they made or lost money based on a single company's perceived performance. With the advent of mutual funds, however, investors could easily spread their money among a variety of companies. They could continue to invest in the stock market but with much less risk of a big downside.

Every business has peaks and valleys. Some fluctuate over intervals of several years, while others vary sharply with the seasons. The higher the peaks and valleys, the greater the risk. In an ideal world, a business plan could assume only an upside in the marketplace. But that rarely happens, and diversification reduces the risks of the downside.

The case study that I am most familiar with is in the home remodeling industry. Many years ago our business was 100 percent dedicated to larger residential remodeling design-build projects. Our processes, people, and product were totally geared to this market and clientele. We began to notice, however, that many of our clients were asking for smaller-scale projects. At first, we had no choice but to turn down these loyal design-build clients because we were not positioned to do smaller jobs effectively. Soon after, a major downturn in the real estate market forced us to look at ways to diversify, and we remembered the increasing demand for smaller projects. The result was the launch of a handyman division that not only serviced our client base and complemented our design-build services but also created new clients and reduced the roller-coaster effect of our basic business model. Since that time (1992), when we were a four-million-dollar local company, we have grown into a $100-million-plus national business with sustainable growth year after year, largely due to being diversified.

Diversification is usually easier when it grows organically out of your business's core competency, but it can also come from sources completely outside the business, such as investing in gold or real estate. When a business is riding high, diversifying is often the last thing on the owner's mind, but it is the best time to diversify because funds are more readily available.

Investing in the future. Investing is a long-term activity that may take many forms. Financial investments are the ones we usually think about—setting aside money for retirement in 401(k) plans or IRAs, or investing in our children's future by saving for college tuition. But we can also invest time and energy, like a new business owner who puts in long hours to ensure the future success of the business. Think about the ways you are investing in anticipation of future changes when it comes to evaluating your company's positioning.

A retail business owner may anticipate needing more space for inventory and commit to a larger lease. Another business may be considering a new type of cash register that can help it remain competitive by moving customers through checkout more quickly. A dental practice that wants to grow and expand will need to invest not only in space but also in staff that has the needed skills.

Remember, as I mentioned earlier, training is an investment, not an expense. This notion forms the basis of a whole new way of thinking about how to position your business for the future. Investments need to be made with people, processes, technologies, and product. It is always tough to properly distribute time, energy, and money between today and the future, but it is harder if you do nothing.

Score This Fitness Key

Like many of the criteria, positioning has many facets. If you apply the concepts I have outlined above, you will not only have a consistent way to look at your company's current positioning, you will begin to think about positioning in the future.

Review each element:

Stable: Is your business consistent and stable (which allows for change with less risk)?

Market awareness: Do you understand your customers? Do you know how larger issues affect your business?

Well-capitalized: Do you have enough capital to support current operations as well as plans for growth?

Diversified: Are all your eggs in one basket?

Investing: Are you investing properly for the future?

Rate your organization on a scale of 1 to 10. (Use decimals if needed.)

Positioning. Write in your score: _____

Alliances

"None of us are as smart as all of us"
- Ken Blanchard

Another criterion that I believe is important to the health of any business is what I call "alliances." These are the most critical relationships you can build outside of your immediate company family.

In our personal lives we understand the importance of friends—people who enjoy each other's company and who can count on each other in times of need. Friends bounce ideas off one another and consult about all kinds of decisions, big and small. If we need a recommendation on which gym to join or which dentist to visit, we ask friends because we have a history with them and we trust their opinions.

Most of us have a similar relationship with our neighbors. The friendship may not be as deep or as strong, but we rely on our neighbors just the same. Sometimes it is a matter of convenience—walking next door for a cup of sugar is easier than driving to the store. Sometimes it is a matter of safety—when we are on vacation, the neighbors keep an eye out for suspicious characters. And sometimes we need a favor—someone to accept delivery of a package. In business, I call these relationships *alliances*, and they may be even more important than they are in our personal lives. The risks are greater in business, and we need alliances to help us make decisions that often affect dozens or even hundreds of people. Having an alliance in business means having a history and sharing a climate of trust. Like our personal friends, we use our alliances to test ideas and to confirm our choices, even to borrow tools.

Allied competitors. Alliances can include businesses that compete in the same market as your company. Although many businesses are conditioned to see anyone outside of their own organization as a stranger or enemy, most businesspeople experience similar kinds of problems. Other business owners are trying to make a living just like you. And like you, they would prefer to be perceived as friends and allies rather than as strangers or enemies.

In fact, one of the more positive conceptual shifts that a healthy business makes is to define its true competition not as the business next door or the Big Box retailers, but as the customers themselves. Many businesses are competing with other priorities in their clients' lives and with their clients' fear of making the wrong decision. Building strong alliances with other businesses can help you meet these competitive challenges.

Long-term relationships. A strong alliance is a long-term relationship, not a short-term one. A strong ally extends himself above and beyond the basic requirements of the relationship when asked. A strong ally supports you even when doing so holds no direct value for him or when the cause is of no interest to him. A business alliance is a professional friend that watches your back and is proactive with helpful information or insights.

An alliance is like a good friendship, except that it is part of the professional arena rather than the personal. A professional alliance is usually rooted in an individual person, but you probably won't know where that person lives or her children's names. A professional alliance may not involve someone you would want as a drinking buddy or dinner guest, but the relationship still goes beyond the usual business interactions.

Regular communication. Alliances are not something you collect like trophies; they are active relationships that should work to the mutual benefit of both parties. That begins with good communication. As with a personal friendship, an alliance can move quickly from good to bad graces, so the relationship should not be taken for granted. A healthy professional alliance needs regular care and feeding for it to be valuable. Regular dialogue can come in many ways. It could be a weekly e-mail exchange, a monthly lunch meeting, or a quarterly visit. The form the communication one takes is less important than its frequency and regularity; otherwise, the professional relationship will drift apart. In a healthy business, regular dialogue with strategic alliances is a priority, and this type of communication is treated with the same importance as with a client or a key staff member.

Mutual benefits. Alliances don't always produce benefits immediately or even in obvious ways. But cultivating alliances increases the opportunities for benefits to develop. Some people appear to be lucky; their businesses just seem to fall into good fortune. Often, however, what appears to be luck or happenstance is actually the result of great effort sustained over a long period of time. People who work hard at building alliances tend to have more opportunities land in their laps. The benefits may start with a simple widening of your circle of influence, as businesses with whom you are building alliances circulate your name among their alliances. You may find yourself invited to participate in a variety of activities—meetings, informal gatherings, working sessions, sporting events—all as a result of your connection to allied businesses. Over time, tangible opportunities will present themselves. You won't know when or how often, but they will appear as if by magic. The true cause, of course, will be that your alliances have worked behind the scenes to help you grow your business and you have become a magnet for their ideas and energy.

It's not enough to have a vague feeling or general sense that you are actively creating and maintaining alliances. You need to quantify it and then go back and measure it by asking specific questions about the scope and strength of these relationships. How often are you communicating with your alliances? What is the best way to reach out to each of them? Do you know the top three priorities for their business in the coming year? Do they know your goals, priorities, and targets? When was the last time you brought all of your alliances together to share your businesses vision for the future? By addressing these questions, you can objectively evaluate whether you have these kinds of relationships.

Today's business environment is more complicated and unpredictable than ever before. You can face your business challenges alone, or you can face them together with other businesspeople who share your goals. I believe that strategic alliances change the dynamics of businesses and give them not only additional bandwidth but also reduce the risks.

Score This Fitness Key

As you think about this element of your business' health, ask these questions: How many ideas have landed on your desk over the last month from alliances? Has the interaction with the alliances been about how you can help them? Are there new team members that have joined you from your alliance network or referral? Did an alliance help you increase revenues or improve the bottom line recently? With these specific questions, you can be honest about both the number of alliances you have as well as the nature of the relationships and the benefits to your business.

Allied competitors: Do you have any established alliances? How many can you name? Are any of them engaged in the same business you are?

Long-term relationships: Do you have long-term business relationships?

Regular communication: Do you meet or otherwise communicate with allied businesses regularly?

Mutual benefits: Can you name synergistic ways you have benefited from strategic business alliances?

How strong are your business alliances? Rate your organization on a scale of 1 to 10. (Use decimals if needed.)

Alliances. Write in your score: _____

Fitness Checkup Summary

"Even if you are on the right track, you'll get run over if you just sit there."
- Will Rogers

The fitness checkup that you have just undergone may be a "first" for your business. And, like the first stress test you ever took, you didn't know what to expect. Now that you've been through it once, I think you'll agree that although the criteria are quite simple, accurate answers require some real reflection.

Surprisingly, the results of the checkup do not vary much for businesses of different sizes—the fundamentals are the same for a $500,000 business as they are for a fifty-million-dollar company. As I explained earlier, however, what does affect the results is the mindset of the person performing the checkup. Before we go any further, I want to make sure that you haven't inadvertently undermined the results.

For instance, I am quite sure that some of you have skimmed through the chapter headings without reading the full descriptions (sometimes businesspeople are not very patient). Or you may have only partially completed the scoring and jumped ahead to look at the results. Some may have been fearful of what the checkup would reveal and, as with a medical exam, may have either withheld important information or painted a picture that is rosier than it should be. Others—I call them "business hypochondriacs"—may have missed the big picture because they were too focused on the details.

If any of these scenarios sounds familiar, now is a good time to return to the checkup to read it more thoroughly and score the criteria more rigorously. Remember, the goal of the checkup is not to pass judgment but to provide a systematic process to evaluate the health of your business, and to create a benchmark you can use to measure progress. How you treat the checkup affects not just the scores for each criterion, it also determines the benefit you will ultimately derive from having gone through the process.

This fitness checkup is also designed to gauge how well your business partners and other key team members are aligned. Throughout my career when delivering this fitness checkup, I have observed that in a healthy business everyone's scores are closely aligned. But in a less-fit business the scores of partners or team members often vary dramatically. If you haven't already asked your co-workers to take the checkup, now would be a good time to reconsider, before we move to an analysis of your checkup score. Business is a team sport, and sharing this process and the results with others is critical to success.

Although I am using a medical metaphor throughout this book, the business fitness checkup differs from a medical checkup in one important way: you are both patient and doctor. That means that both the diagnosis and the prescription for improvement depend on your making some tough calls. Some of your scores may be cause for celebration, but others may point to the need for intensive care. As with the checkup itself, interpretation of the scoring and the suggestions for improvement will only be as good as what you put into them.

Finally, we are conditioned from our years of schooling to think of a test as signaling the end of a class or semester. Our natural tendency is to close the textbook and never return to the subject. And in most cases, we forget what we learned within a few weeks or months.

This checkup is designed to work differently. The first time through, it gives you a snapshot of your business at a particular point in time. But as you make improvements and take the checkup again and again, the snapshots combine to create a movie that makes it easy to see how your business is changing over time. This type of ongoing analysis is critical because businesses are constantly changing. Your market or team members may change for better or worse. Or it may be that the improvements you implement as a result of this checkup cause you to shift your focus away from healthier parts of your business, causing them to slip. Unless you repeat the checkup regularly, your movie will have some blank spots that could conceal growing weaknesses. That's why this fitness checkup should not be memorialized; it should become an active part of your regular planning and assessment.

Total Your Scores

As you worked your way through the checkup, you were asked to record a score for each fitness key. Go back and retrieve those scores, transfer them to this page, and add them up. The total score will serve as the basis for how you use the remainder of this book. Start with the interpretations in the next section, then move on to the chapters on improvement.

Score Each Fitness Key

_____ Knowing Your Numbers (page 48)

_____ Systems and Processes (page 55)

_____ Leadership (page 61)

_____ Team (page 70)

_____ Product or Service (page 77)

_____ Profitability (page 83)

_____ Reputation (page 89)

_____ Stress (page 95)

_____ Positioning (page 102)

_____ Alliances (page 107)

_____ **Your Fitness Checkup Total Score**

What Your Score Means

"No matter what accomplishments you make, somebody helped you."
- Althea Gibson

The ten chapters of the business fitness checkup are designed to help you come up with a score that approximates how healthy your business is in each of ten key areas. If you haven't yet given your business a score for each criterion, do so now and total them up. In a minute we're going to look at what particular scores mean, but first I want to talk a bit about the scoring method itself.

As mentioned earlier, the scoring system has been tested on hundreds of businesses and has never failed to bring some insight about the health and fitness of the business in question. Each business is slightly different, however, as is every business owner, so the scores need to be thought of as a kind of snapshot taken from a particular vantage point. From a different perspective at a different time, the score a business receives might be very different. This is why I so often recommend that business owners ask key team members to take the checkup, then compare scores.

Another factor to keep in mind when reviewing your score is that the age of your business affects some fitness keys more than others. A young business may score high on product and service due to the owner's giving personal attention to every detail, but it may score low on reputation or alliances due to the brief tenure of the business. A newer business also won't have much history, and this will affect the owner's ability to "know the numbers" or to predict profitability. In fact, one might argue that for reasons like these, it will be impossible for a newer business to achieve a top score. Regardless, it does not change the validity of the criteria for a fit and healthy business and the usefulness in creating a fit business.

That said, the scoring system is designed to be a useful diagnostic tool, whether or not independent scores agree, regardless of the age of the business being examined. If you believe your score is correct and agree with my interpretation of what it means, then you are ready for the prescription for improvement. If, on the other hand, you are not confident with your score or you disagree with the interpretation, then you may want to repeat the checkup or solicit a second opinion. If you still end up with conflicting or contradictory scores, you can still benefit from the improvement chapters. In fact, you can use the points of difference to focus your thinking and analysis. Either way, the more open you are to this evaluation, the more useful the scoring system and recommended steps to improvement will be.

Now, on to the analysis of your score. It is only natural that most of you will look first for the scoring range that covers your score. Once you've done that, however, I recommend you read through the interpretations of other scoring ranges both above and below your own. This is particularly helpful if your score is close to the top or bottom of a particular scoring range, where a small change can easily move you up or down a level.

85 or above

If your score is 85 or higher, your business is quite healthy. I would assume that your business is at least five years old. It is unlikely that a young business has achieved such a high level of fitness in such a short time. If your business is younger than that, it could be that very high marks in certain elements of particular fitness keys have overpowered weaker elements. As mentioned earlier, good referrals, high close rates, and low marketing costs may lead the owner of a young company to rate the business high on **Reputation** without giving fair play to other elements that affect that fitness key, such as "respect" or "recruiting." To find out if this is the case, I recommend that you review some of the scores, or ask a team member or advisor to take the checkup and provide a separate score, then compare the two. If the second score is similar to the first, congratulations. You are among a small group of companies that already understands and lives by the principle of constant improvement.

Owners of companies at this level of fitness can probably stop looking over their shoulder and instead invest more time into answering questions such as "How can I gain market share? Are there additional products and services that I can launch? Can I turn up the dial and grow at a faster rate?" An old adage says, "Knowledge instills confidence, confidence creates enthusiasm, and enthusiasm sells." Let the confidence you have gained from knowing that your business is fit and healthy fire up your enthusiasm to grow in new directions.

A score in this range also signals that it is a good time to learn how to look further down the road. Most businesses have a tough time looking beyond a year or two, but a company at this level of fitness has good control over day-to-day operations and can afford to invest some energy into three- and five-year planning. I suggest you begin with a management retreat to carve out some time to think in a focused way about the future of your business. You may want to invite key team members or a consultant to offer additional perspectives.

Owners at this level of fitness can and should delegate more authority to key team members and encourage everyone in the operation to take on more responsibility. If you have not asked other team members to participate in this checkup, then I would encourage it. If they come up with similar results, it will add validation and build confidence. But the odds are that their checkup will differ in some respects, and these differences creates opportunities for dialogue and may help deepen your understanding of important issues.

Keep in mind, however, that with a score of 85 or more, it is easy to forget that your business is not static. It can slip into a lower score relatively easily if you are not continually monitoring performance. This is no time to rest on your laurels. Read the following improvement chapters to see if there are ways you can raise specific scores to even higher levels. Mark your calendar for another checkup six months to one year from now.

75 to 84

This is a good score. As mentioned above, it is a good idea to determine the extent to which the age of your business affects your score, and to make the corresponding adjustments.

Otherwise, a business with a score in this range is sitting on a solid foundation. The fundamentals are in place, and much of the hard work has already been done. The main question to ask is "Why is the business good but not great?" The key is to figure out what has to happen to move the fitness score up from this range to the next. It is also worth considering what could happen to cause the score to slip one range lower.

I generally find that there are a couple of common denominators for businesses that score in this range. The first is a strong team score. Most businesses in this range have some strong individual team members, loyal people with talent, and a strong work ethic. There may be some work to do on systems and other elements, but the business has the talent needed to move it up a notch.

The second common denominator is that businesses in this range have a great product or service. You can probably confirm this by listening to your clients and industry experts, even to prospective clients who opted not to do business with you. But a quality product is only one piece of the fitness formula, and in some other important respects, your business is not quite there. If you are a newer business, it could be said that you have potential; but more mature businesses should heed what an old friend of mine once said on this issue: "At some point, being told that you have potential becomes an insult." What you do with your potential is what matters now.

As you study the upcoming chapters on improvements, you will discover many ways to continue to move toward greatness. The key is patience. At these higher levels, change is more incremental. The bar moves, but only an inch at a time.

65 to 74

A score in this range is a wake-up call that requires action. I spoke earlier about preventive maintenance, and that's the situation of businesses in this range. A few problems in critical areas threaten to do more damage if they aren't repaired quickly and in the right way. But there is no time to lose and you need to take action soon; the changes cannot be put off until the next fiscal year. Sometimes it is difficult to appreciate the urgency of your circumstances because you might not immediately see the consequences.

However, you will see them soon enough if you leave matters to take care of themselves. But don't take my word for it—get a second opinion by asking your spouse or a key team member to take the checkup for your business. Compare the results for specific criteria to see where they align and where they don't. In many cases, a second pair of eyes and ears can help you ask the right questions and move forward at the right pace.

Assuming that a second score is within a few points of the first, focus first on any score below 5. These are areas that need immediate attention just to keep you from slipping back a level. This may be difficult because human nature is to improve upon areas where we already excel. In this case, however, you can't afford to lose time improving something you already perform reasonably well. To get the job done, you may have to delegate authority to someone on your team to ensure that these critical issues get the attention they deserve. This doesn't mean that you are out of the picture—far from it—but you are removing the temptation to procrastinate or ignore troublesome areas that are acknowledged weaknesses.

By concentrating on scores below 5, you will not only put a finger in the dike, but you will also engage your best opportunity for improvement. It is much easier to move a 4 to a 6 than is it to move a 7 to an 8. Concentrating on scores below 5 is like picking apples off the ground before exerting the effort to climb the tree. Plus, the incremental success you will enjoy from immediate improvements will give you the encouragement you need to take on more difficult challenges.

As you read through the improvement chapters, break the recommended remedies into three groups: things you already know, things you think you understand but are not sure will help, and things that you can most easily accomplish. Attend to the last group first, then direct energy toward gaining a better grasp on the middle group.

50 to 64

A business in this range has entered into the danger zone. It is not a point of no return, but it is more than just a casual wake-up call. To extend the analogy to a physical checkup, this business needs strong medicine, and failure to adhere to the recommended regimen could be life threatening. Some business owners need to hit this level before they can commit to improvement; the brink is what motivates them to take action. Others simply aren't aware there is a problem until they expose it using a tool like this checkup. Either way, changing behavior and developing healthy habits is one of the most challenging things anyone can do, whether it has to do with personal health or business health. But in circumstances like these, you have no choice.

Two points are key for businesses with scores in this range. First, you must act immediately. Second, knee-jerk reactions will only make your problems worse, so it essential that you follow a rational process to make the necessary changes. The last half of this book is devoted to helping you accomplish just that.

Odds are you have uncovered weaknesses in several areas, so you should begin by soliciting help from your team. You need both buy-in from others as well as their eyes and ears, because it will be difficult to climb out of this hole by yourself. If you have several team members who you feel are vested in the health of the business, invite them to participate in the improvement process; if your company is smaller, get everyone involved. This won't be easy, especially if you are someone who has always carried the leadership load on your back. It is difficult to discuss serious business problems openly and, most importantly, to listen to others for answers. But a score in this range demands that you make the effort, no matter how uncomfortable you may feel.

Once the team is up to speed on the issues, you will want to bring in an advisor or consultant to assist you and your team in the move to a healthier place. It is unlikely you will improve without outside help. The good news is that I know of many businesses that have reached this point and turned things around. The key is to act now!

35 to 49

Your business is in critical condition. If this was a physical checkup, your doctor would be admitting you directly into the hospital to undergo further testing and possible surgery before the night is out. The circumstances are dire. Everything else needs to be placed on the backburner. This is no time for keeping secrets either, but you might want to delay sharing the results with your team until you have had time to think about where to begin. Cool heads should prevail and, as difficult as it is to be optimistic in the face of such serious problems, a negative attitude will produce negative results. The thing to remember is that whatever the issues are, there is a process for addressing them.

More than 60 percent of small businesses fail within the first five years in part because the owners do not realize how serious their problems are. You no longer have that luxury, and you now can choose between becoming a statistic or transforming your business into a success story. If you choose to improve, a strong first step is to bring in a financial specialist, followed by a business consultant or even a business friend to help you explore specific issues. A good business coach may not have all the answers, but he or she will guide you through the maze by helping you focus on the right questions.

Recovery will require an investment of both time and money, and both may be scarce at the moment. But the result of the soul searching, testing, and advice should be a plan focused first on stabilization, then on improvement. This plan needs to be set out in writing, and it should include milestones to be reached over relatively short periods of time. The plan also needs to be monitored at regular short intervals until the business is out of danger. You should enlist the help of your advisors as part of the monitoring regimen to ensure that you stay on course. Eventually, your team needs to buy in to the plan as well. You may need to provide incentives for their extra efforts as milestones are met.

less than 35

With a score this low, you want to look first at the age of the business. For a very young business, a low score is not necessarily a serious issue, and the upcoming chapters on improvement will be very useful. Next you want to review the checkup to make sure that no mistakes were made in scoring. If the score still remains the same and you are the owner of a business that has been around for five years or more, you need to answer some hard questions: "Why did I get into this business in the first place? What do I like, the business or the vocation? How does this business affect others?"

As we discussed in an earlier chapter, most businesses have evolved from one individual's passion for a particular vocation or idea. At first it may have been recreational, then a part-time way to earn extra money. At some point, whether deliberately or through the force of its own momentum, the owner discovered that he or she was in business. Unfortunately, in most cases the original passion was focused on the craft—the product or service—not on "business" per se. To be successful over the long haul, you need to find passion in business and not just the craft. Business is a game, with rules and strategies that you can learn and master. As with other games, it is hard to maintain discipline if you don't love what you are doing. Is being in business something you love, or are you stuck in it? Is your business a straitjacket that keeps you from realizing your true calling?

If this describes your situation, you may find that going to work for someone else is the best solution. It may rekindle your passion, and because someone else will be shouldering the business responsibilities, you may even be able to take your passion and your skill to a new level.

A score this low also means that your business is probably adversely affecting others as well. Would some of your loyal team members find more opportunity in another organization? Are you working such long hours that you have little time left for your family?

Sometimes, the most convincing evidence that the business is not working is to look at the owner's income. Do you know how much money you are really making? Many small business owners don't because they don't take into account all of the extra hours they put into the business working nights and weekends. I often point out to people in this predicament that they can make more money working substantially fewer hours and with less liability if they go to work for someone else. In most cases, they will also spend most of their time doing the things they love to do, the things that got them into the business in the first place. Most react as if I am trying to sell them a used car, but when they actually sit down and do the math, they usually discover that their true earnings are below that of their own hourly employees.

If this description fits, folding your tent may be the smartest move you can make. Some of the most successful, happiest, and most masterful people I know do not run their own businesses. They are able to channel their passion and energy under another organization's umbrella. Not only are they more fulfilled but so are their key team members, vendors, and clients.

In a later chapter we will discuss some tips and strategies to consider when exiting your business. In the meantime, acknowledge that these are difficult decisions that should always be made after reflection and after seeking the opinions of reliable advisors.

Next Steps

"I feel like the greatest reward for doing is the opportunity to do more."
- Dr. Jonas Salk

You have now reached one of those "moments of truth." Now that you have completed the fitness checkup, the question is, where should you go from here? The answer depends not only on the results themselves but on how you feel about them and what you think about the process that has brought you this far. The checkup is a test, and most of us feel some anxiety about tests and have mixed emotions about the results. Much of this discomfort stems, I suspect, from our earliest school experiences when tests were not voluntary and served to determine whether we passed or failed.

Fortunately, this test is different. For one thing, from the outset the entire process has been voluntary. Obviously, something caught your interest early on and spurred you to read this far. Now that you're here, you can regard it as an end or as a beginning. It can serve to confirm what you already knew, or it can act as a wake-up call to what remains to be learned. It can be a one-time thing or it can represent the first step of many in a long progression.

At this stage in the process, your emotions may very well be mixed. Quite naturally, you are probably happy about your good scores and disappointed or anxious, even angry, about your poor ones. You may have been energized by the process and flooded with new ideas, or you may be questioning what you've read and wondering whether some of the concepts even apply to your business.

Regardless of how you are feeling, you have a decision to make. As I see it, people who complete the checkup fall into one of three categories: skeptics, seekers, or implementers. Let's look at each one to see where you fit.

Skeptics. Readers who react with skepticism usually believe that their businesses are unique and that the concept of business fitness is a waste of time. If you are feeling that way, consider this: I have never met a business owner for whom this process was not relevant. I have seen many businesses crash and burn, and each time the reason was based in one or more of the criteria I have put into the checkup. I am certain that if at some point before their demise they had not only completed the checkup but had initiated what I call the right improvement, many would still be in business.

Also, the idea of a checkup may not be as compelling as the notion of improvement, which is addressed in the coming sections. By continuing this process, skeptics may find something that strikes a chord. Often, a single, small idea can ignite whole new ways of thinking.

Seekers. Another reaction is one of curiosity and belongs to people I call *seekers*. They typically find the checkup process interesting and intellectually stimulating and, happy with the bits of insight they have already gained, they are curious to learn what other tidbits might pop up. Although they may not have had any "Aha!" moments yet, they feel the breakthrough may be just around the next corner, and that the coming chapters contain the pot of gold at the end of the rainbow. If you fit this description, it is perfectly fine to treat the balance of this book as you would an *a la cart* menu, selecting those ideas that seem most satisfying. However, you may want to pass the book over to others on your team who may have the appetite, if you will, to complete the full course.

Implementers. The third type of reader is more practically minded. If you are among this group, you are probably feeling a need to learn more about what the results of the fitness checkup mean, and you are eager to fulfill the prescription for improvement. In fact, some of you may become so obsessed with new ideas and plans for improvement that you alienate those around you. (I can be like that at times—just ask my wife.) The good news is that there is nothing to lose and much to gain by forging ahead. The key is to control your pace to give those around you time to become aligned with your passion.

For some of you, elements of all three of these types may be present. What is critical, however, is that you recognize that the ten criteria I have presented are tools that allow you to view the true current state of your business. In the coming chapters, I will help you understand your scores and show you how to move from where you are to where you want to be. The ultimate goal is to begin to see the stock rise in your business. For some, making the necessary changes will be a long and sometimes painful process, but well worth it in the end. For others, it may be a simple matter of making a few easy tweaks that embellish an already pretty picture. Remember, you will gain the most benefit if you approach the following chapters in the right frame of mind. Successful, healthy business owners know that a commitment to constant improvement is what keeps their companies in shape, separates them from the competition, and allows them to grow.

Thomas Jefferson said, "We will be judged not on our ideas or concepts but by our actions." It is time now to take action!

Part Three:

Improving Your Business

Preparing To Improve

"If you think you can or you think you can't, you're right."
- Henry Ford

Most people make New Year's resolutions, and most people fail to keep them. When I've asked audiences about this during speaking engagements, I usually find that it's not because the resolution was stupid or unrealistic. So what happened?

Your business depends on your increasing the odds of succeeding. If you focus on why you have succeeded or failed in the past, I think you will find it generally boils down to a few things.

Motivation. The things we have the greatest success changing are the ones with really strong "whys." For example, you may be fifty pounds overweight. Your clothing is tight and uncomfortable, and when you look in the mirror you are not thrilled about what you see. But at dinner you have an extra helping of potatoes and the apple pie. You know that by eating these things you will not lose weight and may even add a pound or two, but you think, "There is always tomorrow."

Now imagine that you go to the doctor and, after he reviews your blood work and performs a stress test, he announces that your cholesterol levels are off the chart and he's worried you may have heart issues. Now your weight problem is a wake-up call. Pushing away from the table is not just about your vanity and your wardrobe, it is about survival.

Before I initiate changes, I always create a written plan that begins with the reason I need the improvement to happen and the consequences if it does not. The simple act of writing down the pros and cons is often enough to give you the conviction it takes to commit to change.

Context. Creating an environment conducive to improvement increases the likelihood of success. A simple example might be catching up on reading. Most people who would like to read one book a month, whether for business or pleasure, are frustrated because, given a busy work schedule, it's hard to find the time to sit down and read on a regular basis. Or else they make several false starts so that they end up reading parts of the same book two or three times. But when these same people get away on vacation, they are able to read a book almost every day. How so? The difference is that the context or environment has changed, becoming friendlier to their goals.

To make business improvements, you need to create a supportive environment. That usually begins with changes in how your workweek is organized. Look for opportunities to eliminate some activities or change their time and frequency. Switch to communication via e-mail when it's more efficient. Most of all, be more proactive and less reactive. Decide which part of the day is most productive for you and make an appointment with yourself (yes, just like you would set a lunch date with a client) to work on your improvement. If you're still having trouble, try planning a brief getaway retreat.

System. In the fitness checkup, we discussed why your business needs strong systems to be healthy and grow. The same is true when it comes to making improvements. Most improvement occurs incrementally over a period of time, so monitoring progress in a systematic way is critical.

Going back to the example of New Year's resolutions, we fail not only because we don't have well-articulated reasons but also because we do not have an improvement system. Without a process, our resolutions are just a to-do list. We put a lot of energy into declaring the resolution and telling everyone about it, but little effort goes into creating a process that will make the resolution happen.

A process or system needs a written plan that includes milestones tied to specific dates, a regular commitment of time and, most importantly, a consistent way to monitor progress. Just as a pilot monitors a plane's progress and makes hundreds of adjustments during each flight to ensure a safe arrival at his destination, you need to "watch the gauges" to make sure you are following your "flight plan" for improvement.

Having the discipline to monitor progress regularly is where most people come up short. To avoid falling into this trap, map out a weekly checkup on progress and record the results in writing. This is no different from dieters who get on the scales at the same time each week and record their weight. If you see improvement according to plan, great; if not, figure out what went wrong and make the adjustment so that next week you will be back on track.

Clarity. Being clear about the task at hand is, in itself, a powerful thing. The clearer you are about what it is you want to accomplish, the more you will stay on track and not get distracted. I find that clarity of purpose is easier to achieve when I make the effort to imagine it in as much detail as possible.

As a cyclist, I go through the process I am talking about every time I prepare for a major ride. To improve my odds for success, it helps me if I am very clear about as many elements and details of this ride as possible. Will the course be hilly or flat? What will the weather be like and how will it affect the road surface and my comfort? What will I have to give up while training for the race, and how will that affect my normal routine? To help with my motivation, I try to imagine how I will celebrate my accomplishment. I also try to name other benefits, like weight loss, that will come out of reaching this goal.

By painting a detailed picture of what you want to achieve and what it will take to achieve it, you will not only find clarity, but you will raise questions that will help you prepare your improvement plan. By asking *who, what, when, where, and how,* you will put your lens in sharp focus on the goal.

Commitment. Common sense says that, whenever you set out to make a change, you should be careful not to "burn your bridges" just in case things don't work out. But I recommend just the opposite. Making a complete and unequivocal commitment to your goal increases the chances that you will do what needs to be done to reach it. One simple technique to ensure that there is no going back is simply to tell everyone you know what it is you are trying to accomplish. This kind of "bridge burning" will make it more painful to quit, and may give you additional motivation to stick with it.

I used this trick myself while writing this book. Instead of writing the book first, then approaching a publisher, I did the opposite and signed a publishing contract with a hard deadline for delivery of the manuscript. That commitment provided me with added motivation to make writing a priority even on days when the words wouldn't come easily. I also began telling friends and key team members about the book, and shared the concepts and the deadlines. They not only became cheerleaders (and we all need cheerleaders), they also held me accountable to the process. By making it harder to fail than to succeed, you increase the odds you will stick with your plan.

Pace. It makes a difference how fast you attempt to make an improvement. If you want to lose twenty-five pounds before a big event, such as a wedding, you may need to go on a crash diet. This may not be the best tactic for long-term health, but it will help you to look great for the wedding photos. If, on the other hand, your doctor asked you to lose twenty-five pounds to improve your overall health, you might set a more gradual pace with tweaks in diet and exercise.

As I mentioned earlier, I like a pace that is aggressive but realistic. It forces me to take into account other priorities in the context making the desired improvements. And it's a concept that I can use to help align team members. Finding the right pace for the improvement process will increase the likelihood that I will stick to it.

Manage the change. People process and accept change at different rates and in different ways. As a business leader, you need to keep your eye on the goal and the potential benefit to the business, and not worry about the egos. I first understood the importance of this concept about ten years ago when a key team member was killed in a car accident. The loss was a huge blow to our company, but I could not understand why everyone was not expressing the same level of sadness that I was feeling. We brought in a grief counselor, and she said something that I will never forget: "Don't judge others on how they process death. Some will need to cry, some will need to laugh, some will be silent, but some will need to talk. They each have their own way of relieving the pain."

Not everyone is going to embrace your plans for improvement. There are many great ideas collecting dust on the shelf because not everyone was committed to the cause and no one in management thought team buy-in was a priority. Some of your key team members will need to come to the need for the improvement on their own, maybe not until they experience some pain firsthand. But change is not a one-size-fits-all proposition. Try not to judge people on how they process change. Instead, give them some time to come to the idea on their own. Often, individuals who resist change fear consequences, real or imagined, and simply need time to regain their perspective. In other cases, there may be something you overlooked that will have a strong effect on a particular individual. You'll get better results if you face the issue squarely rather than try to ram through your plan no matter what.

I have faced this issue in my own business. Several years ago, we wanted to elevate a certain individual to a leadership position within a team. However, this team had worked together for a long time and were not comfortable with strangers in their camp, least of all a new manager. We began by integrating him into the team's activities gradually over a period of several months. We invented reasons for him to work with some of the individuals on the team to help break the ice and build greater rapport. Eventually, the interactions generated mutual respect, and we introduced small leadership responsibilities but without any title change or formal announcements. By the time the day of the formal promotion arrived, the transition was seamless because the new team had already bought into the change. Had we not managed this change so carefully, we would probably have had some negative fallout and maybe even a mutiny.

It is important to be mentally, physically, and emotionally ready for improvement. You can change for the better if you have a plan, a system to help you measure progress, and the conviction to carry it through.

Improving Your Numbers

"Ninety percent of this game is half mental."
- Yogi Berra

Improvement in this category is more about discipline than skill or intelligence. It begins with developing good habits, not focusing on mastery. Once you have the fundamentals down, you can inch your proficiency higher and higher.

This fitness key underlies all of the others. Improving in this category alone won't move your business closer to the Promised Land, but it will substantially reduce risks.

Your vital numbers. Successful businesspeople can tell you what the three to five vital numbers are in their world. In the remodeling business, they are number of leads, total sales revenue, gross profit percentage, overhead, and percentage of completion. If these vital remodeling statistics are strong, net profit will be strong.

If you are thinking that there are many more numbers that are critical to your business and need to be watched, I won't argue with you. But having lots of numbers to look at has little value if you are not able to keep track of them all. Because the key here is to develop a routine that includes close monitoring of these vital statistics, it's important that you are not overwhelmed. To successfully improve in this area, I recommend that you pick three to five to focus on. You can expand the number later, after you are more comfortable with the routine.

Don't keep your vital numbers a secret; make them an integral part of your team culture. Make tracking your vital numbers a part of the agenda for every staff meeting, and find an appropriate place to post your vital numbers regularly for everyone to see. Find creative ways to keep your vital numbers a priority with your team by weaving them into contests or competitions, making them your mantra, theme, or rallying cry. Your team may need a little time to catch up with your new focus, so be patient. It may take months for the light bulbs to go off, but eventually they will if you have the discipline to stick with it.

Guiding your business with numbers. Knowing your vital numbers is only the first step; actively using those numbers to make business decisions is a habit that all successful businesspeople develop. If you need to improve in this area, one place to start is to make it a point to review your vital metrics more frequently than you have in the past. For example, if you have typically waited for your accountant to review your numbers each quarter, then shorten the cycle and meet monthly instead. If you are already conducting this kind of review each month, you may want to ask your bookkeeper or CFO to give you a report each week. Be careful, though, to make small adjustments. The goal is to develop new habits that you can stick with. Just as a crash diet doesn't generate lasting results, making too extreme a change compared with what you have done in the past may backfire.

Including your company's vital metrics in everyday decisions about staff, products and services, marketing, and other aspects of your business may be a big cultural shift for you, and even greater shift for those around you. Even when everyone understands intellectually what needs to be done, making it part of their day is not so easy. One way to develop a healthy habit is to make appointments with yourself to focus on this practice. If you treat these appointments with the same importance as a client meeting, within thirty days you will find yourself routinely filtering all business decisions through the lens provided by your key numbers. Your goal is not to become robotic or mechanical but to begin to wear a different shade of lens in your sunglasses. What you see and how you react will be different. If a pilot were just one percent off course when flying from NY to LA, he would land in San Francisco. Use these vitals to guide you.

Reviewing your numbers. Once you know your numbers and have learned to use them to guide your decisions, the next level of mastery or improvement is finding the right frequency for examining them. This is more a matter of rhythm than of time management.

To begin, break your dashboard into three time intervals—daily, weekly, and monthly—then assign key metrics to each. Some metrics will be in all three categories, but the level of detail may vary in each timeframe. For example, you may want to track sales in three different ways: a daily report comparing sales to date vs. monthly projections, a weekly report that adds a comparison to previous months, and a monthly report that adds a comparison of sales totals vs. year-to-date projections as well as the status of each individual salesperson. By investing five to ten minutes each day, thirty to sixty minutes each week, two to three hours each month, you will be able to make the small adjustments in a timely fashion. It is much easier to make more frequent incremental changes than to make big moves that are disruptive and require a lot of damage control.

Many people ask me where they will find the time for these exercises. The answer is that these proactive measures will result in not just better overall fitness and health, but also more available time. Most business owners spend a great deal of time reacting to problems that seem to come out of nowhere. If you devote three or four hours each month to these improvements, I guarantee you will free up twice that much time simply because your business will function more smoothly.

Understanding the basic financial tools. Let's face it: most people got into business because they had a passion and an aptitude for a product or service, and not to become accountants. They like money, but mostly earning it or spending it, not keeping track of it. Unfortunately, to stay in business—and certainly to improve and grow—you need to become more literate in financial management. Without this basic skill, you are handicapped, like a carpenter who only knows how to use a hammer. To build anything, he has to rely on others to measure and cut. I recommend that you approach this task in baby steps so it will not seem so daunting. Who knows, you may even find it rewarding, if not actually enjoyable. Mostly, though, it will make a big difference to your business fitness.

Begin this exercise by taking your accountant to a working lunch. Treat this get-together as a seminar, and don't be afraid to ask lots of questions. Ask your accountant to walk you through the three to five financial tools that he or she believes are critical for you to monitor. For each one, ask your accountant to identify the three to five numbers you should look at first. Make sure you understand how the numbers relate to each other, and how changes in one affect the others. Use a live copy of your company's accounts, and ask for two or three improvements you can make immediately. This meeting should fill sixty to ninety minutes, and the final order of business will be to arrange a follow-up in two to four weeks to monitor progress. I think you will find that your accountant will be inspired by your attention; this level of interest is rare. That will likely lead to more suggestions and eventually into a situation where your accountant becomes a true partner in your success.

Once you have the basics under way, you should consider joining a business group or meeting informally with another business owner. Begin a dialog about what financial tools she uses and what she considers to be her key metrics. There is more than one way to skin a cat—you never know where the next good idea will come from. I learned this many years ago, while comparing business insights with a friend from Oklahoma who was also in the remodeling business. We were talking about ways of measuring company performance, and he said the goal was to maximize the returns you get from each of your carpenters. It sounds sort of obvious, but I had never heard the idea before. In the remodeling industry, most business owners look at total sales and gross profit percentages, but they do not calculate any kind of per person return on investment. As it happens, this way of looking at things is wonderfully useful. For instance, a carpenter working on a twenty-thousand-dollar project for five weeks generates four thousand dollars per week, while a carpenter working on a one-hundred-thousand-dollar project for ten weeks generates ten thousand dollars per week. By looking at productivity numbers this way, a remodeler can learn to choose projects that promise better returns while also adjusting margins to be more competitive if required.

Creating and tracking a budget. If you do not have a budget for your business, you are not alone; many, perhaps most, business owners don't. And of those who do, only a few track that budget effectively. While it is possible to get by for a while on intuition and good fortune, owners who operate without a budget are flying blind. With no flight plan, you have no way of knowing where you are headed until you get there. That destination is usually a year-end financial report, which for many is the first time they discover whether or not they made any money.

The news is not always bleak. Yes, many business owners think they are doing great when the reality is that they are losing ground every day. But the opposite may also be true. You may be lying awake at night, tossing and turning with worry that you are risking too much, when your finances are actually in good shape.

The only way to avoid either extreme is to first build a budget, and then check it at regular intervals. A budget is a dynamic business tool that helps you keep your bearings. Tracking it is as important as creating it, and this is where most fall short.

Start with something simple. Use a standard budgeting form or software that your accountant recommends. In fact, you may want to retain him or her to get you set up initially. Highlight the items that you know for certain, and make note of those you are predicting. In some cases, you may need to work or manipulate the budget by running some "what-if" scenarios. Try at first to keep the number of variables to a minimum. This process is much easier than you think. Generally, about 80 percent of the budget numbers can be plugged in with little effort based on your history; this means that most of your time can be used on the remaining 20 percent that require more thought.

For example, you probably know or can easily find monthly or yearly totals for office rent, utilities, insurance, and many other fixed overhead items. Once those "givens" are out of the way, you can devote more thought and analysis to variables like how much you should budget for marketing or technology improvements. Think through not only what you want to spend this year but also whether you can pay for everything out of cash flow. Will you have to finance some initiatives? Your accountant can help, but ultimately you need to understand this process yourself. Who knows, it might be fun, like a game or jigsaw puzzle. The more interesting you make it, the more engaged you will become. That leads to better understanding and eventually to better business fitness.

Once everything is set up, monitor actual performance against budgeted performance, item by item. Finding the right tracking cycle is important. Monthly profit and loss statements are common in most industries, so this is a good place to start. Make an appointment with yourself to spend about an hour reviewing the budget. Meet with your accountant, if necessary, until you feel confident that you can interpret the reports on your own. Each month, follow up with adjustments to your planned course. Ask your key team members to follow the same process and make them accountable, not only for the results, but also for keeping you plugged into any variations to the original plan.

The more routine this review process becomes, the less painful and more useful it will be. By starting with baby steps, you will see gradual improvement over a fairly short period of time.

Knowing your historical numbers. As businesses get healthier, they get wiser and use all the tools at their disposal to plan and predict. When I was younger, I believed that what we did in the past had little value for predicting the future. I could not have been more wrong. I now know that historical performance, while not infallible, is the most useful tool we have to predict future performance. But it is impossible to draw on historical data unless you invest a little time to collect and organize it.

Again, begin simply. Go back three, four, or five years and compare your vital statistics, whatever you have determined them to be. Map any trends you see and evaluate the cause of any major fluctuations as objectively as possible. Then use this information as a filter for your budgeting process. My goal is always to make sure that my budget is "aggressive but realistic" relative to history. If you have little or no data of your own, then you may want to use benchmarks from your industry as a starting point. The goal is to improve your knowledge, which will lead to better decisions, more predictability, and a healthier business.

Making sales projections is a good example of how historical data can be useful. Projecting sales revenue can be a crapshoot, but by using past data, you can reduce risk. Many years ago, it was our practice to ask individual salespeople to predict the next year's sales revenue. Some were very optimistic, possibly because they were coming off an exceptionally good month when we asked for their projection; but we found that when we used these numbers by the following year end, actual revenue was all over the place—and usually below what we had budgeted. It didn't take too many experiences like this for us to change our process. We still asked for their best estimate, but we checked it against their prior three-year history. Within a very short time, we reduced actual-to-budget variance from 20 percent swings to less than five percent.

Improving in this category may seem impossible at first, so attack it in stages. If your score was below 5 in this fitness key, then I recommend that you block out a chunk of time each week (maybe on the weekend) to move the bar forward. If your score is 6 or 7, then pick three "low-hanging apples" from everything I've mentioned and focus there. Scores above 8 are ready to move toward mastery. This may include introducing financial management concepts to key team members.

Improving Systems and Processes

"Whenever you are asked if you can do a job, tell 'em, 'Certainly, I can!' Then get busy and find out how to do it."

- Theodore Roosevelt

For the free spirit, the very idea of systems and processes conjures up an image of a rigid, mechanical, militaristic approach that stifles creativity. For the analytical thinker, on the other hand, these words are music to their ears, bringing to mind the notion of efficiency, orderly conduct, and logical activity. For analytical types, focusing on systems and processes is the highlight of their day; for free spirits, it is a source of dread.

Everyone has a place on the continuum between these two extremes, but the most successful business owners are in balance, located somewhere near the midway point. They appreciate the value of systems and processes, but they do not become a slave to them. They understand that almost everything we do is a series of systems and process, some simple and obvious (like running errands) and some more complex (like flying a 747). Finally, most systems and processes in business are dynamic. They require regular review so that as the market changes and personnel shifts, systems and processes are realigned.

As we look at the following ideas for improvement in this area, keep two things in mind. First, there is a process to improve your processes. And second, developing a system-oriented culture may end up being more difficult than developing the system itself. Improvement in this area will be slower than you might expect, so be patient but diligent.

Writing down processes and systems. As I noted in the checkup, most business are more a product of evolution than design. As a result, many critical business functions are not written down or recorded in any way. The first step to developing a system-oriented culture is to try to articulate what you do and how you do it. This can be in narrative form or a diagram or flow chart; it can be printed and compiled in a binder or it can be a series of electronic files; it can even be a series of videos with voice-over narration if that suits the particular process better. The point is to record what gets done and how.

This may be difficult at first, but the very act of creating a written record enables you to see things that you now take for granted. It may help reveal weak links that need preventive maintenance or areas that require a complete overhaul. Creating a written record can also highlight areas where everyone is in sync and areas where there is chaos. You might also uncover redundancy and overlaps. Any one of these results will improve your businesses fitness; taken together they can have a substantial effect on every aspect of your operation.

Start slowly by picking something you feel you know well, like your sales process. Chronicle every step in the process, beginning with a customer inquiry and the initial contact, then moving to the first appointment and finally to the follow-up or close. Record every detail no matter how insignificant it may seem—one benefit of this exercise is discovering some of the little things that make a big difference in the outcome.

Sometimes, looking closely at one process suggests the next step. Writing down your sales process leads naturally to recording your perceptions of your client's experience. What are each of the steps from their points of view? How do they react to what you do? Do you control the experience or do they? What opportunities exist to gain further loyalty and do additional business with your clients?

Choose the three to five most important processes to start with, then move on from there. Writing everything down may seem like a lot of trouble, but in my experience most businesses find it surprising and very fruitful. When you are done, rather than a blank canvas you will have a framework that you can manipulate to improve your business. You will know where your business is effective and well understood, as well as places into which you need to shine more light.

Individual personalities. A business that is a product of evolution may be guided more by personalities than processes. There are certainly some advantages to this, especially in the early stages when the skills of a company founder may be essential to its product or service. Some companies never abandon this model and remain successful. But I believe they are self-limiting in their ability to grow and to adjust to changing market conditions. This applies not only to company owners but also to most other positions in a company. If job descriptions and responsibilities are defined in terms of the individual currently holding the job, I believe the business is at risk and is limited in its ability to grow and adapt.

It is important to have all-star players on your team, of course, but the issue is whether they are determining how the game is played. To find the answer, first take inventory. Outspoken or flamboyant team members often attract early attention during this exercise, but what you are really looking for is an individual with specialized skills, as well as for habits or patterns among team members that have not been examined in a long time. By asking the right questions and being open-minded and objective, you may find some interesting nuggets that pop out in this area.

You will likely uncover two kinds of situations. In one case, you may find that an entire aspect of your business is completely dependent on the skills of a single individual. This also means that your business is limited by the skills that person lacks, and is vulnerable to changes in that individual's personal circumstances. In this case, you will want to revisit several job descriptions to ensure that critical responsibilities are shared. You might also introduce cross training so that several individuals become competent in the necessary skills. Finally, you may decide to reexamine the business itself to see if this particular function can be accomplished with less risk by some alternative means.

The other situation is one in which processes are in place, but a particular individual is ignoring or short-circuiting them, or has gradually fallen out of sync with them. Changing technology, for example, may create an issue. You may have a hardworking but old school employee who is afraid of office technology, even simple e-mail. Being out of his comfort zone, he tends to find a way around any process that requires technology. Although he may get high marks from all your clients and may be loved and respected by the team, his non-compliance can create problems that might seem trivial today but will affect future initiatives.

It may be enough to instigate a conversation with the individual in question. I have found that many times, these people are as unaware of the situation as you were before you took a closer look, and just raising the subject is enough to change behavior. In other cases, they won't respond positively or there will be contributing issues that are irreconcilable. In that event, you have three choices: 1) do nothing and live with it; 2) look for a creative "win–win" solution; or 3) terminate them. Living with the problem is unacceptable in almost any situation, and while letting a team member go is always a last resort, sometimes it is unavoidable. I usually encourage people to exhaust the search for win-win solutions before taking this more drastic action. You might transfer the individual to another position that leverages her skills but does not adversely affect in-place systems. Or you might tweak the process in exchange for specific adjustments on her side.

An example of how this might play out can easily occur with something as simple as new company attire. Many companies require team members to wear uniforms or logo attire as part of an overall effort to extend the company brand and keep an edge in its public image. Attire is, however, an area that some believe crosses the line between the personal and professional realms, and certain individuals will resist any initiative in this area. A forceful "my way or the highway" approach might work in some cases, but top performers and very popular team members present a difficult challenge. If you think explaining the business reasons behind the clothing requirement will not be enough to turn the tide, consider involving these people up-front in the attire selection. It might make the change more of a non-event.

Keep in mind that improvement in this area is not a matter of judging anyone personally. The goal is to get everyone on the team aligned with the company processes and systems. As with any change, there may be some short-term pain, but there will also be long-term gain and better business health.

Communication vehicles. Because communication needs will change dramatically as your business grows, check your systems annually. It is best to make changes early and stay ahead of the curve.

A good place to start improving communication is to record your communication structure, just as you would any critical system. By diagramming the communication process that presently exists in your organization, you should be able to identify its strengths and weaknesses. Also, communication technology has made great strides in a very short time, so it is important to make sure that your methods are keeping up with the times.

In our company, for example, we have created a simple but effective way to communicate called "Case in a Minute." It was inspired by a local TV station that provides a news update called "Sports in a Minute," which communicates all of the important sports highlights of the day in sixty seconds. We put this idea together with the fact that all of our office and field personnel have cell phones, at the time a fairly recent development. Every week I record a simple, one-minute message that covers key metrics, team member highlights, important dates, and so on. Team members receive a recorded voice message each week. The whole thing takes about ten minutes to prepare, but it touches more than three hundred people in just one minute. Not only is it important because of what the message contains, it improves the team spirit, too.

There are many ways to communicate: print and electronic newsletters, direct mail client updates, key metric reports, lunchroom postings, and so on. More important than the means of communication, however, is a way of measuring and ensuring its effectiveness.

There is usually no need to turn a communication system upside down. But you will see your business performance improve after implementing even a few small changes. These will lead to others in a natural progression that doesn't create much fallout.

Commitment to training. When times are tough, it is tempting to eliminate activities like training because it doesn't always generate immediate returns or easily measured results. However, a commitment to training is a good indicator of a healthy business, not only because of the direct benefits to team performance, but also because it indicates that the leadership understands and values the long-term benefits.

Improving your commitment to training begins with renewed appreciation for all of its benefits. As a first step, make a list of everything that can be achieved through training. Some, like improved efficiency or fewer errors, are obvious and come readily to mind; other benefits, like increased employee retention or pride in accomplishment, are less quantifiable but no less real. Making this list may be the most important step you take because it will give you the conviction you need to make training a priority. Every time I have performed this analysis, I have always come to the same conclusion: training is an investment, not an expense.

The next step is to take inventory on your existing training programs, whether formal or informal. As you think about where to begin improvements, you may want to solicit feedback from team members. Often, because they are plugged into day-to-day operations directly, their ideas are practical and insightful and can give you the best read on the training opportunity. Additionally, if you make them a part of the process, the likelihood for success will increase.

Determine three areas of your business that could benefit most from training and begin with a few pilot programs to test the water. They can be small, stand-alone events or brief sessions woven into standing meetings. Listen for feedback, make adjustments, and be patient: creating a culture of constant improvement takes time. It may be several months before team members open up enough to interact with each other in a way that will bestow the full benefit of training.

If you think that's the case, then ease into it. For example, if you have a weekly staff meeting or specific sales or production meetings, begin by devoting fifteen to twenty minutes to improvement. Simply transferring information is not enough; discuss a hot topic that challenges attendees, or engage in role-playing. Over time, they will begin to see the benefit of this part of the meeting and will even look forward to it. As it gains momentum, it may even grow into a larger program. Years ago, we had a weekly sales meeting into which we wove some simple sales training. Based on the positive results and feedback, we began conducting monthly sales mastery workshops, as well as weekly sales clinic webcasts that are now available on demand.

It is also important not to go overboard with training. Half an hour per week is appropriate in the beginning, especially if the training addresses crucial business activities, such as sales, marketing, or people skills. Other good beginning topics can be more general in focus, such as time management or CPR training.

Once you have an established training culture, you can take it further by offering internal certifications or setting up a corporate university. But don't get ahead of yourself; build a proper foundation first. Invite constant feedback on content, format, and frequency, and modulate progress accordingly. Training that misses the mark can easily lose its effectiveness and cease to deliver on the investment.

You may also want to try using outside trainers or creating an annual training allowance for team members to use at their discretion. These kinds of programs often return twice on the investment, once on the actual training and once on the increased employee loyalty and improved morale.

Team evaluation processes. As an owner or business leader, when was the last time someone reviewed your performance? Have you ever had even one such review while in business? Probably not. When you don't experience the benefits of a performance evaluation directly, it is difficult to appreciate its importance for others. Even if you have an evaluation system in place, the process is probably inconsistent and overly complicated, and therefore, ineffective. One way to tell is to observe employee attitudes. Do they think of evaluations as a trip to the candy store or a visit to the dentist?

Approaches to performance evaluation vary widely. Some are stiff and legalistic, while others are more casual. Some are directly tied into compensation and others keep salary discussions separate. Some companies use different processes for different types of job descriptions. Whatever your current system is, you will benefit from the most immediate improvement if you ensure that the evaluations are performed regularly and in a consistent and uniform manner. No one will take an evaluation system seriously if it occurs intermittently. At our company, everyone is evaluated no less than once each year, and less formal quarterly review meetings are strongly encouraged.

Set expectations among your team members. I personally conduct reviews with senior management. They know that when we sit down formally, we will discuss their role, specific contributions, personal style, areas for growth, and so on. I deliberately separate the evaluation process from any discussion of compensation. This reduces stress a little and makes for a more constructive conversation.

Improving Leadership

"Leadership, like coaching, is fighting for the hearts and souls of men and getting them to believe in you."
- Eddie Robinson

Strong business leadership is a skill that must be mastered as well as a mindset and a way of thinking that becomes part of your business culture. The demands on leaders and the style of leadership needed will also vary dramatically based on the size and complexity of the business. Leading a workforce of hundreds located in several satellite offices is very different from leading half a dozen centrally located employees.

To improve your leadership score, focus on easy, short-term exercises that lead to success habits that you can gradually leverage into long-term gains. The leadership improvement ideas presented here follow the sequence of the fitness checkup; you can move through them in order or jump straight to the section that most interests you.

A clear purpose. A common attribute among businesses with strong leadership is a clear sense of purpose. Business is complex in the sense that it has many parts and pieces, but it need not be complicated. Strong leaders acknowledge the complexity but recognize that a simplified approach makes it easier to get everyone aligned. The first step in this process is to boil down all of a business's complexities until what is left is its essence, and out of this comes a clear purpose.

Because the word *remodeling* is part of our company name, many people assume that our purpose is to build additions or remodel kitchens and baths. Those projects are, in fact, a major part of what we do, but our true boiled-down purpose is to help homeowners solve problems and realize their dreams. Whether or not we end up undertaking a project, every time we interact with a homeowner, we create a client. With enough clients, projects will follow. This distinction is not semantics. It is a mindset that influences our business decisions and our behavior.

There are lots of ways to "boil down" your business and find its purpose. The first step is to stop thinking only in terms of your product or service and begin to focus on the many steps you go through to create it. Engage team members in the exercise, then compare lists and see what appears most frequently. Odds are that somewhere in that shorter list is an action that best describes your purpose.

Another approach is to solicit customer feedback. Either create a customer satisfaction survey or review those you have already collected, and be sure to pay close attention to the answers to open-ended questions. When customers answer questions like "What did you like best about our company?" or "What is the most memorable part of your interaction with our company?" they tend to zero in on the one thing your company does that makes the most difference in their lives. Somewhere in the list of the terms that show up most often in these surveys is a clear statement of your company's purpose.

Once you have determined your purpose, make it your mantra. Recite it daily, mount it in a frame on your office wall, create a computer screensaver, and discuss it with your team. Use your clear purpose to develop a simple mission statement that you can use to communicate with your team and, through marketing materials, to your potential customers. Get into the habit of looking at decisions through the filter of your business purpose, and use it to resolve conflicts. Your business purpose will sustain you and your team in tough times, and will become the rallying cry for growth.

Vision. Leadership vision is not an option; it comes with the territory. Your team and your clients look to your company's leaders to provide both short- and long-term vision and direction, and the key to success is in balancing the two.

For most business leaders, particularly those still actively involved in day-to-day operations, the biggest challenge is finding time to step back and take a broader view. A simple but effective technique is to make appointments with yourself. This may sound a little contrived because most business owners are programmed to put practical, hands-on matters first in line, ahead of seemingly non-productive activities like planning. So don't over-think, just set up a one-hour appointment once or twice each week and see what happens. Just as you would for an appointment with anyone, jot down a few questions you would like to answer and issues you would like to address. In some cases, it will help to remove yourself from the day-to-day distractions; that can be as easy as closing your door for an hour, but it may require something more deliberate, like reserving a table for one at your favorite café. The point is to ensure that the time is yours to spend without interruption. It will take real effort at first and will take some getting used to—kind of like taking up jogging for the first time. But be patient and begin slowly. In a matter of a few weeks, you will find this planning time can be both refreshing and invigorating. Once you have created this new success habit, not only will your short- and long-term planning and vision improve, but your day-to-day responsibilities will also benefit because you will be looking through different eyes.

Leadership is accountable for vision. It is what everyone in the company looks to the leadership to provide. It is what sustains morale and inspires achievement in turbulent times.

Communication. Effective leadership communication is a mindset. Without it, few things are accomplished effectively. In fact, many great ideas never get off the ground because of ineffective communication.

As I coach future leaders, I find that they are often focused on finding good solutions to business problems but without thinking through how these solutions should be communicated. When I push for answers, they usually come up with good ones, but the real challenge is to get to the point at which thinking through how a business decision will be communicated is as important as the decision itself. Will communication be more effective if it is directed to everyone in a single message, or is it preferable to tell a few and let the news filter through to others? Does the decision require a preemptive message, or will getting consensus and buy-in be more effective? Are there key individuals who should be told before others? Will any damage control be required?

It is easy to downplay the importance of effective leadership communication, but if you can improve in this area it can mean the difference between success and failure. If you are uncomfortable presenting to more than a handful of people, taking a public speaking class will certainly help. But it is secondary to the central idea of making communication an essential part of every business decision you make. If what you decide is always accompanied by a plan for who should be told, as well as when and how they should be told, you are on your way to inching up your fitness score on this fitness key.

Respect. Respect is not a characteristic you receive from someone you've just met. Respect takes time. Here are three elements that you can focus on to improve this area.

Empathy. Respect for leadership is impossible without empathy for team members and what they are up against in both their professional and personal lives. Caring genuinely about a client's pain or joy resonates beyond the walls of the business and leaves a positive lasting impression.

Listening. Sometimes people just need someone to listen. The key to good listening is making a concerted effort to suppress your need to solve problems or defend positions. Instead, simply open yourself to what people want to communicate. While that's not particularly easy for many type-A personalities, it pays dividends. Over time, you will find that the better you listen the more people will tell you. This is the key to success in any selling situation, and when team members feel comfortable about speaking their minds, it gives you additional perspective on important internal issues. Ultimately, of course, good listening is irrelevant if it does not lead to actions. Respect grows from the perception that a leader listens carefully and acts thoughtfully on what he or she hears.

Walk your talk. A leader who behaves as if he or she is exempt from the rules that apply to everyone else on the team will never be respected. This is a particularly critical issue today because media coverage of corporate scandals has predisposed many in the rank and file to think that company leaders break the rules all the time. For that reason, your business leadership needs to go overboard in its efforts to color between the lines and behave in a way that clearly communicates that there is no place for special treatment. Better yet, don't keep your commitment to this policy a secret; emphasize it at every opportunity. Most importantly, be prepared to enforce it regardless of the consequences.

Leadership improvement is a process. Sometimes it is a matter of recognizing new patterns or developing new habits; at other times it means adopting a new perspective. Some of you may find the improvement process to be natural and easy while others will struggle mightily every step of the way. Those in the first group must resist the tendency to become complacent, which leads to backsliding; those in the second need to be patient and committed to inching their way to gradual improvement. In both cases, the effort will pay off many times over.

Improving Your Team

"A championship team is a team of champions."
- Unknown

Retention. Retaining the most valuable members of your team is a long-term process. Perhaps the best place to begin is to look more closely at the reasons people leave your company. Are they running away from something? (Studies have shown most workers leave their jobs because they do not like, respect, or work well with an immediate supervisor.) Or is it a case of a cherry-picking competitor and, if so, what is it about the new offer that makes it so attractive? In most cases, you will uncover a variety of reasons for employee attrition, but try to see past individual cases to the systemic reasons behind it.

The other side of the coin is what you do to motivate team members to stay with *you*. Begin by developing a simple employee survey to help you get a truer perspective on how your team is feeling. Make it anonymous so that employees feel safe expressing their true opinions. Ask about the particulars of their job, but also include questions about the work environment, co-workers, benefit packages, and other factors that influence employee attitudes.

The performance evaluation process is another opportunity to explore this topic. During your one-on-one conversations, be sure to move beyond discussion of day-to-day projects and ask about employee aspirations. More than ever before, team members today want to be challenged and provided with new opportunities, and if they can't find them in your organization, they will seek them elsewhere.

This is another reason I am so bullish on growth. Steady growth provides more than increased market share and healthy profits, although those are certainly important. It also creates opportunity for your team. Opportunity is the magnet that will keep good employees with you and keep them focused on your business.

In addition to making sure the environment is conducive to retaining key team members, you need to evaluate the monetary aspect, too. Whether you call it "profit sharing" or the more colorful "golden handcuffs," the concept is the same: giving your team a stake in the success of the enterprise builds loyalty.

When you initiate a profit-sharing program, start slowly and be careful to not give away too much too fast. If you believe that your profit margins are predictable, then it might work well to distribute a percentage of year-end profits. One way to do this that has been successful in our company is to distribute quarterly advances. This delivers the incentive at a point closer to when it was earned, which is a better motivator (if profit varies from what was predicted, you can reconcile everything at year end). As you become comfortable with this type of incentive-based relationship, you might consider a deferred compensation package that gets paid out in the future (don't try to figure this out for yourself; consult with a financial advisor).

The rules of thumb that I always follow are: 1) keep it simple—if employees have trouble understanding the incentive program, then it will fail; 2) start with a baby step and build for the longer term; 3) keep it a top priority (with a quarterly distribution, as mentioned, or perhaps just a quarterly report or an occasional discussion); and 4) include the team—inviting the beneficiaries into the process of creation ensures buy-in and makes the outcome a win-win.

Top performers. In athletics, it is easy to spot top performers. They are the ones who are featured in the highlight reels and who are at the top of the salary structure. Spotting the top performers on your team is almost as easy, but spotting those with the potential to be top performers is a bit more difficult. Approach the issue systematically by trying to identify team members as A-, B-, or C-players, using input from managers if possible. If, after completing this simple assessment, you find that less than 20 percent of your team falls into the A- list, you have two choices. The first is to focus on specific B- or C- players and create a plan to move them up a notch. The alternative is to recruit from outside your company for new talent. This exercise will also force you to think about how you define top performance.

Top performers are often a double-edged sword. They raise the bar for everyone they work with, but they also can be high maintenance employees. A great team, in business and athletics, needs all-stars but also strong bench players. I believe at least 20 percent of your team should be top performers, but you need to balance these individuals with others who are satisfied to be role players.

Managing and motivating top performers can be difficult. Be creative without corrupting your policies against special treatment. Our company calls on top performers to teach others, a strategy that delivers twice the benefit because it not only improves the performance of the students but also motivates the teachers to new levels of achievement.

Top performers need new challenges, but you also need to keep them focused on producing for you. Great companies and great teams achieve this balance.

Gung ho attitude. Improving attitude is more of a cultural change than a quick fix situation. A gung ho attitude begins at the top and sends the message that failure is not an option. Attitude should be part of your screening process when building your team. There is a tendency to focus on specific skill sets and to ignore attitude. As mentioned earlier, I think that three questions about job candidates are central to the hiring process: Can they do the job? Will they do the job? Will they fit? Two of these questions have nothing to do with competence, but have everything to do with attitude.

As a leader, you need to be on the lookout for changes in your team's attitude. If you feel it slipping, then try one or more of the following suggestions:

Change the pattern. Try adjusting a meeting agenda to focus not on the "stuff" of day-to-day operations but on more subjective issues that might be affecting attitude. You may even want to meet one-on-one or in a different setting—whatever it takes to uncover the underlying causes. Sometimes it is enough just to provide a forum in which people can air out what is on their minds.

Focus on "them." Bring in an outside speaker or give each team member a motivational book to read or tape to listen to. Then organize a session where people can share the feelings and ideas they gained while reading or listening.

Invest your time. It is difficult to know how much time to invest here, but it is better to invest too much than too little. And in challenging economic times, it will need to be a much higher percentage of your time than on sunnier days.

We have had success improving attitudes by pairing gung ho individuals with others who are less positive.

Gung ho attitude is something that ebbs and flows, so you need to watch the factors that may influence it. It could be affected by a tough business environment, by too fast a pace or unrealistic expectations, by a difficult client, or by an imbalance of work loads. When you see attitude eroding, find the reason and release the pressure as quickly as possible. Balancing hard work with empathy or balancing high expectations with a fun work environment can go a long way toward establishing a permanent cultural change.

Commitment to constant improvement. Improvement in this area will rest on two criteria: 1) your ability to create an environment that is conducive to constant improvement, and 2) the internalization of this principle by the team members themselves.

The dedication to a proper environment for constant improvement flows from the core belief that "training is an investment, not an expense." By creating opportunities, you are investing in your team, and you expect a return on that investment. Make this commitment clear to your team, and draw attention to the investment you are making at every opportunity. If your choices and decisions are visibly influenced by this investment and the expected returns, others on your team will begin to think the same way.

Likewise, as you see individuals taking advantage of training and education opportunities, don't keep it a secret. Let everyone know that you think these behaviors are important, and reward team members who participate. At our company, for instance, we celebrate an individual team member's participation in training by highlighting them in a staff meeting and in the company newsletter. Also, make your commitment to training a part of the annual performance evaluation process. Use this review to identify areas of improvement and to suggest training options. If your industry has sanctioned certifications, create a structured way for your team to pursue them. For example, you might create an education allowance that pays for the cost of the certification class if they pass or earn a certain grade or better. Having an additional "stripe" creates a sense of pride and accomplishment in team members that is worth its weight in gold.

The second step toward establishing a culture of constant improvement—one in which the individual becomes the driver—is more difficult to create. It may help to think of the commitment to improvement as an eternal flame, and your job is to make sure it does not go out. That means keeping abreast of all learning opportunities your team is involved with, whether they are company-initiated or privately pursued, and celebrating them. It means feeding the improvement fire with a constant stream of ideas and resources that they can grab on their own.

When individuals move beyond being practitioners or "mechanics" to a level of mastery where they become a student of their vocation, your improvement investment begins to yield huge returns. Not everyone takes advantage of the opportunity. I will typically "toss" an improvement "ball" to an individual and wait to see what happens. They don't always hit it out of the park (although some do), but if they take a swing at it, I follow with another. If they don't take a cut at it, I count that as one strike. They will only get three, and if they don't try to do anything with the opportunities, then I know that they are not committed to constant improvement.

Your future leaders. When I get into discussions with a management team member about possible business opportunities, the first question I generally ask is "Who will lead this charge?" Without the proper leader, most ideas will never come to fruition.

Developing future leaders for your business is another long-term process so, odd as it may sound, the best time to identify and nurture leaders is when you don't need them. This may create an uncomfortable feeling for some business owners who have a difficult time with the thought of actively moving individuals into position to take over their job. But I have found that the only way for me to move forward is if I develop others who will push me into new passages.

The critical first step is to identify individuals with leadership potential. Next, verify that your assessment is correct and matches their ambitions, and make sure they are committed to your business and to their own leadership development. Our process begins with a blend of basic analysis and team member interaction. A question I always ask is "If Bob (a manager) were hit by a bus, what would we do?" This then leads to questions like "Who is Bob's backup?" "Is Jim (Bob's backup) prepared to step in?" "What needs to be done to better prepare Jim?" "Is Bob aligned with and supportive of Jim's improvement?" and so on. Simply by asking these questions, you will find the voids in their leadership readiness, and you can begin to fill them.

In an effort to take a timeout from the day-to-day activities, we also developed a monthly leadership workshop. During this ninety-minute gathering, the group discusses leadership issues that are common to all of them. This gives them an opportunity to stretch and strengthen leadership muscles that don't often get used in their regular positions. They also discuss other businesses, read and discuss business books, and practice presenting to each other on a variety of subjects.

Ideally, these discussions take place in good times when the pace of progress can be more leisurely. Occasionally, you will need to make a "field promotion," possibly in the face of a challenging market or difficult client. If you have identified the right individuals, you may be surprised at how readily they will step up to the challenge if they know that you have earmarked them for advancement.

These future leaders are your crown jewels. Investing time and money in them promises maximum return. Find time to meet with them (in person or via conference call) weekly for thirty to sixty minutes. In these meetings, focus more on their growth than on day-to-day issues. Find mentors both inside and outside your company, and identify educational programs to help them improve. Most importantly, toss leadership challenges their way to help them test their new muscles, but be careful to plan three to twelve months in advance. This will give you time for damage control measures, if necessary, and help to make the transition natural and seamless.

Exceeding expectations. These two words can make the difference between success and failure, between an average team and a great team. Nine out of ten business challenges could be overcome if everyone on your team exceeded expectations. Imagine for a minute that your team consistently exceeded expectations. In our business, it would mean projects always coming in under budget and ahead of schedule, craftsmanship of the highest quality, delighted clients, and an endless stream of referrals. Profits would improve, retention rates would be higher, and our company would be a very happy place to work.

In the course of leading business culture training for the last ten years, I have found that the concept of exceeding expectations is difficult to pull off. One aide I use in my teaching is to get people thinking about the effects of exceeding expectations by just one percent.

For example, if you tell a client that you will call him at one p.m. and you call him at one fifteen, you are late. He may interpret that as your being an inconsiderate person who doesn't value his time and won't value his business either. If you call him at twelve fifty-nine, however, then you are on time, which he may interpret as your being someone who is on top of your game, who can be trusted, and who really wants this relationship to be successful. This night and day difference in impression on the client is the result of simply exceeding the expectation by one minute. The effects are the same with team members and vendors, too.

Another technique is to ask a team member who consistently exceeds expectations to share her thoughts on the subject with others. Make sure that the emphasis is not so much on what was actually accomplished, but rather on how it met or exceeded expectations.

Our company adopted a theme many years ago that helps team members to align themselves with expectations. We call it "aggressive but realistic," and although I've used it earlier in this book when discussing a pace, it can apply to almost any situation. I like it because it is non-threatening in a way that reassures people that they won't be asked to perform beyond their capacity, but it also inspires them to push to the limit. It is amazing how a simple theme like this can spread into every corner of a company's operations, to the point that everyone now uses it to set expectations.

Stepping up accountability. We all know that we should be accountable for our promises, for our roles on the team, and for hitting key milestones. It doesn't take any special training to understand what this means, but it does take some effort to practice it day in and day out, in a variety of circumstances. Unless you can create a culture of accountability among your team and an environment in which everyone reinforces the concept of accountability by their actions, then starting any initiative will be like dragging a bag of rocks up hill.

A good first step is to start a conversation. Don't assume that everyone's ideas about accountability are the same. Conduct open discussions of what accountability means in the context of your business, and emphasize how its effects ripple through the company. Make it a point to address the pain of falling short and the joy of hitting the mark.

Another key is to grant authority. After you have alignment on what it means to be accountable, give your team license to do what is necessary. Unless they have the power to correct errors and do the right thing, preaching about accountability will fall on deaf ears. For example, if a project manager is accountable for hitting a specific time deadline, he needs to be free to manipulate his budget to allow for overtime work. In the case of a salesperson who is accountable for meeting a revenue goal, he may need to have the freedom to offer certain incentives to entice the customer to close the deal.

Accountability in business is similar to accountability in a family but could be arguably more critical to the business's success. Begin by defining accountability both at a global level and in their specific role. You might want to survey your team to determine the clarity of their accountability. Based on these results, develop a plan for training and communication. Make accountability a priority issue and include it in staff meetings. Develop a system to monitor your progress at both an objective and subjective level. After about six months really take inventory and see if this has made a difference on not only key metrics but also morale of your team.

If you believe "people are your greatest assets," then make them and their improvement a priority. The improvements outlined above may seem overwhelming when taken as a whole. But if you make a genuine effort to inch each one forward at a reasonable pace, you will see the results in the health and fitness of your team and ultimately of your overall businesses success.

Improving Product or Service

"He profits most who serves best."
- Arthur F. Sheldon

Little things matter when it comes to improving your product or service. Today, clients judge your business based not only on what you do and how well you do it but on the way doing business with you makes them feel. What differentiates a business today is its ability to deliver its product or service in a manner that leaves a lasting positive impression with the consumer about the entire experience.

As you shift your focus to this aspect of your business's health, keep in mind that small improvements in each distinct element of this fitness key will make an immediate and tangible impact in your overall business health.

Being well defined. In your fitness checkup, you were asked to determine whether or not your product or service is well defined. Here are three simple exercises that will help you improve your score.

First, gather one or two years' worth of data about your present client base and the products or services you have delivered during that period. Organize the results into categories based on factors such as size of transaction, client demographic, geographic location, and profitability. Include subjective categories as well, such as how easy a client was to work with or how a transaction affected team morale. In our remodeling business, for example, we ask our team members about their preferences. Some like building additions while others prefer doing smaller projects with shorter start-to-completion cycles. Similarly, some prefer to work with our clients that are doctors while others like the detailed orientation of our engineer clients.

Next, analyze this information to flush out any patterns. You might find, for example, that transactions of a certain size generate 10 percent to 20 percent more profit than larger or smaller transactions. Or, you might discover that client satisfaction ratings vary dramatically based on the length of time involved in the transaction. You may even discover that certain team members affect profitability or time to market.

I remember a time many years ago when our company had two designers selling remodeling projects. Based on their comments and the enthusiasm they expressed for certain clients, I assumed that one excelled with younger clients and the other with older clients, so that is how I parceled out the leads. After analyzing the sales data, however, I found that the opposite was true: the close rate for the one who I thought worked effectively with younger clients was much higher when he worked with more mature clients, and vice versa. If I hadn't found the pattern, I would never have changed the way I distributed leads. Not only did the change increase sales and profitability, it made for a happier sales team.

Finally, use what you learn to develop a plan that targets the kind of business that you want to pursue. In many businesses, transaction patterns develop more by accident than by design or plan. In the remodeling business, for example, many young companies pursue projects with a larger selling price without, however, understanding lost opportunity costs or how scale affects profitability. This may work well until the market changes and project sizes shrink, at which point total project dollar value may no longer be a reliable indicator of success.

The alternative is to understand the effect of as many of the inputs to a transaction as possible. Use this information, first, to educate your team on the concept of the "right client" and "right product," then to shift the emphasis and direction of your marketing efforts to hone in on your sweet spot. Being clear about your target will increase the odds of hitting it.

This process should be methodical and deliberate. Test your theories by changing one thing at a time and monitoring the results. Progress will be incremental, but you will move toward better overall business health and fitness.

On time delivery. Deficiencies in this area are easy to recognize but challenging to fix. The first step is to define what the consequences of failure to deliver on time really are for your business. Begin by creating two lists, one for all the effects when delivery is on time and one for all the effects when it is not. The "on time" list might include things like delighted client, less stress on your team, more profit, increased efficiency, better productivity, and improved referrals. The "not on time" column might include things like increased complaints, more cancellations, production bottlenecks, and delayed payment. Comparing these lists should give you the motivation you need to make certain that "on time delivery" is a priority.

In my experience, both within our organization and with other companies, the challenge to improving on time performance typically begins with the expectations that we set with our clients. Most clients have a preconceived notion about how quickly something can be completed or delivered. Regardless of how far off the mark they are, we often lack the courage to educate or correct them for fear of losing the sale or starting off on the wrong foot. In many cases, this is the result of allowing a craftsmen or a frontline worker to set the expectation without adequately training her about the consequences of being late.

Training will help, but to be effective you as the leader of your company must clearly communicate what your tolerance level is. If you set a hard and fast rule, your team needs to understand whether or not you are willing to risk losing some business when client expectations for delivery time don't meet that rule. And your team needs to know what kinds of exceptions to the rule, if any, are allowable. Monitor progress based both on hard data and client perception. If you can improve in this area, both your reputation and your bottom line will benefit.

Quality of the advice. It's easy to be dismissive on this topic because every businessperson considers himself to be an expert and, as such, incapable of giving anything but good advice. But many consumers would disagree. They would say that most businesses are more interested in selling them something than in listening to their problem and helping them solve it.

The best advice stems from the purest, most unselfish motivation. There is no hidden agenda, just a genuine effort to help. As I have mentioned elsewhere, I strongly believe that, even when the advice does not lead to a sale, it creates a client. The short-term gain may be lost, but the long-term benefit is invaluable.

Before you jump to the conclusion that your team always delivers quality advice, do some testing. Set up a few simple scenarios and ask your team to role-play. Alternatively, shadow some of your team members as they interact with customers. In either case, evaluate not only the specific advice but also the tone and the manner in which it is offered. Is the business well represented during the interaction? Does your company culture shine through? Do salespeople give different advice than members from your operations team?

Training can really help you and your team to improve these skills. Regular internal workshops conducted by your top performers are a good place to start, but you may want to engage a third-party trainer as well. Remember, the advice being delivered defines your business in your clients' eyes. It is often the basis of the first interaction consumers have with your company, and getting it right leaves a lasting impression.

A well-crafted product or service. One good way to get your arms around this issue is to listen to your team. Create a survey that asks questions about quality vs. expectations and value vs. cost. One technique is to set up comparisons that match your product or service against well-known brands outside of your industry. For example, set up a multiple-choice question that asks team members to select the car manufacturer that most parallels your product or service. Another question might list retail brands and ask respondents to select the one whose quality and pricing is most like that of your company. Now ask clients to complete the same survey. Look at the results of each survey separately but also compare them to each other.

If you have constructed the survey carefully, you should get a good idea of how highly regarded the quality of your product or service is. But the obvious disconnects can be especially revealing. If, for example, your salesperson thinks the business is most like a Mercedes but your production person selects a Yugo, you have a quality issue. Likewise, if your team thinks they are most like Neiman Marcus but your clients point to Wal-Mart, you have learned something valuable about client expectations and the quality you are delivering.

Another type of survey examines quality in a linear way, beginning with the first impression the client may have from a marketing piece through the first point of human contact then to the transaction itself and any follow-up. Each of these steps represent what Tom Connellan, author of *Inside the Magic Kingdom,* calls "moments of truth" when clients make judgments about quality. Make sure that you are at least meeting client expectations at every stage. But go to work immediately to improve areas with low scores. Quality is a fundamental issue, and if you score poorly here you may lose the client forever.

Responding to diverse economic conditions. A healthy business is stable and better able to control both its product offering and its growth. There will always be fluctuations in market conditions, but stable businesses can usually smooth out the curves.

To improve in this area, you need to look regularly at both the threats and opportunities facing your business. Begin by listing all of the external factors that affect your business. What is the natural business cycle—is it seasonal or does it change in five- or ten-year increments? Are you or your suppliers affected by weather patterns? Are fluctuations in raw materials predictable or capricious? Is the labor force growing or shrinking? Factors like these can have either a positive or negative affect, and by keeping tabs on them at regular intervals, you will be better able to predict when the tide is turning.

Down markets represent the most obvious threats, so it is worth exploring some "what if" scenarios. How will your product offer change? How will client requirements change? Is there a counter-cyclical demand that you could be addressing? Are you able to adjust your marketing, product offering, and systems to accommodate these potential changes?

Another useful exercise is to draw a simple pie chart and segment your existing business in terms of various product or service offerings or your targeted market. This is very much like looking at a portfolio that shows how investments are allocated (so much in equities, so much in bonds, so much in cash). Then draw another pie chart that represents how the allocation would look in a down market. The challenge is to create a plan that adjusts marketing, product, and systems to bridge the gap between the two. The best time to plan for a down market is in an up market, but the reverse is also true. Always think about how you might gain market share when everyone else is hunkering down to weather the storm.

If finding time to spend during the week on these issues is difficult, consider organizing a half-day or full-day retreat. Invite key team members and get away from the day-to-day routine to brainstorm these questions. How much of what you decide you are able to act on is, in some respects, secondary to the exercise itself. By simply asking the right questions, you will be much better prepared to fend off any threats that come your way and to take advantage of any opportunities that present themselves.

Improving predictability. Data drives improvement in this area. If you are not keeping track of key business metrics affecting costs, schedule, profitability, and quality, the first step is to improve your mastery of your numbers, as already discussed.

Assuming you have the data, focus on where results are most unpredictable and begin to ask why the variations exist. What factors influence a predictable outcome? It could be that your team requires more training or better supervision or up-to-date tools or technology. It could be that communication with your client is less than ideal or is variable in some way. Or it might be that outside factors, such as vendors, subcontractors, or regulatory agencies have an unpredictable effect on your operations. The heavy lifting is in the analysis, which will reveal where the challenges exist. Making the actual adjustments is generally the easy part.

Changing your product or service is difficult. You need to take a methodical approach, communicate expectations clearly, and get team buy-in. And you need the discipline to monitor any changes. Otherwise, the natural tendency is to gravitate back to where you started.

Improving Profitability

"The measure of success is not whether you have a tough problem to deal with, but whether it's the same problem you had last year."
- John Foster Dulles

Profit is something you can calculate using a mathematical formula. Profitability is a mindset or way of thinking about profit. Better understanding of profit as an outcome requires a closer look at all of the factors and behaviors that affect profitability. Some insights will come simply from looking at profit and profitability from a different angle; other keys to improvement have more to do with maintaining discipline and practicing good habits.

Defining profit. Believe it or not, the fitness scores of most businesses could increase by one point simply from adopting a consistent definition of profit. Ask ten people for a definition and you get ten different answers. It's like having a conversation in which everyone is speaking a different language. Without a translator, there is no alignment around what anyone is trying to communicate.

Begin by creating a pie chart with three main sections: one for cost of goods sold, one for overhead expenses, and one for net profit. In each section, make a list of everything that belongs in that category. Most of the inconsistencies will spring from the overhead

177

category, especially with regard to owner compensation. In small family-owned businesses, a spouse often contributes unpaid labor to the company by keeping the books or working around the office, but these expenses are never included anywhere in cost of goods sold or in overhead. If you are unsure of what all of the components are and where they belong, sit down with your accountant or financial advisor and listen to what he or she has to say. Quite apart from how these inputs affect your taxes, it is impossible to gauge the financial health of your company if you are not accounting for all revenues and all expenses.

Once you have the definitions clear in your own mind, it is important to communicate the concept of profit to others on your team. I have found that repeating the pie chart exercise can really help your team understand the mathematics. Most employees understand the basic idea of cost of goods, but overhead can be a challenge, partly because, depending on their job description, they may not be aware of all of the elements that contribute to the calculation. The pie chart is effective because it illustrates quite graphically how fragile the thin small slice of pie is that represents net profit. It is even more effective when it becomes clear that this small slice has to cover taxes, capital investments, and cash reserves before the holiday bonuses can be paid. How open you are with your financial information depends upon your comfort level. But however much you disclose, just make sure everyone understands all of the terminology and the basic mathematical relationships. Otherwise, a small misunderstanding can create big problems.

Predictable profits. Again, profit is an outcome, but it is also a scorecard. Like good athletes, businesspeople need to be able to predict outcomes. If you take the time to learn to predict all of the individual factors that affect profit, you will improve in your ability to predict profit itself.

You will often find that one component may need to be outperforming its budget to make up for a shortfall in another. For example, if you are predicting that you will need to increase a marketing budget to achieve sales goals, then you may also need to adjust productions levels upward to preserve profit margins.

For some, predicting profit is a game of "what if" that they enjoy playing. For others, it may seem pointless and stressful. Unfortunately, profit is too important to ignore. Remember, you don't have to like everything you do, you just have to do it. But the better you do it, the healthier your business will be.

Seeing profits improve. It may be unrealistic to expect profits to improve year after year, but without setting consistent growth as a goal, it is too easy for profits to slip. There are many variables that can not be controlled; those that can be adjusted need to be kept clearly in sight. If generating improved profits is a top priority, your overall results will be better regardless of external circumstances. If nothing else, try to avoid big swings in profit from year to year. This kind of rollercoaster ride generally means that some element of production or overhead is not performing as expected and you are not reacting strongly enough to get it back in line. Often, this stems from a failure to monitor performance regularly. If you don't know where your profit is headed until your accountant does your taxes at the end of the year, then you need to improve your monitoring cycles. To see consistent profits, you need to make the right decisions at the right time. It may be that you need to cut some weak players or ask others to step up and fill the gaps. Or you may want to invest a little more in marketing to fill the pipeline to hit sales targets. With profit margins being so tight (three percent to 10 percent on average for most businesses), many small adjustments can make a difference of a couple of points.

Keeping short- and long-term in balance. When there is a frenzy of business in your industry, it is generally easy to invest in the future. Likewise, when there is scarcity, most businesses hunker down and focus on the present. Both reactions may feel natural, but they are too shortsighted.

Difficult as it may be, a business needs to evaluate its present condition in terms of what the future is likely to bring.

No one has a crystal ball, but predicting the future isn't as difficult as it sounds if you operate according to a set of guiding principles and long-term goals. If you are always thinking two or three years ahead, you have a better chance to make short-term decisions that will contribute to long-term results.

Profitability is the judge and jury of business. You can't survive without profit, and you can't thrive unless profit is stable and predictable. Profitability is best achieved by focusing on all the factors that contribute to the outcome. If the parts and pieces are all on track and healthy, profit will take care of itself.

Improving Reputation

"There are no shortcuts to any place worth going."
- Beverly Sills

Do you know what people say about your business? Is it positive or negative? Or do they have no opinion because they don't know you? Reputation is the sum total of how the world outside perceives your company and what your team believes and communicates both in words and deeds. Although one or the other may be more important at any given time, both are essential. Improving either one is a long-term process, but there are some simple fixes that will get immediate results. Like a crash diet, however, immediate changes will not become permanent unless you ultimately focus on overall fitness.

Sphere of influence. Think of your business as sitting at the center of a series of concentric circles. Each "ring" represents another layer or realm in your company's "sphere of influence." Closest to the center are your clients, vendors, and subcontractors; in the next layer is the local business community; farther out is your state or regional community, and at the very outside is the national and in some cases global community.

Ask yourself how well those in each circle know your business and how your reputation changes in each layer of the sphere of influence. Many business owners that think their companies are well known are surprised to discover that they don't show up on many radar screens at all. It is also often the case that a company has a better reputation regionally or nationally than it does locally, or vice versa. It may be that the business is perceived to be average in its local market but gets higher marks regionally or nationally because of a special program or charity in which it participates. Whatever the reasons, the key is to understand how well your business is known and how people's opinions change depending on how they interact with you or where they get their information about you.

To become more visible outside your inner circle, look for ways to leverage your alliances and participate in business associations. If time permits, try to become more active in these groups. You may not only improve your reputation but also your leadership skills.

Charitable causes. Aligning your business with charitable and educational causes will automatically expand your sphere of influence, particularly among your client base. (Political causes are more volatile, and can have a polarizing effect on your reputation.) You don't need to abandon your day job, but these kinds of activities will demand a certain amount of your time. One alternative is to invite interested team members to represent your company in some of these causes. Not only will this boost your reputation in the community, it will cause your team to feel better about the business knowing that you care about something besides making money.

A business theme that our company lives by is "If you give, you get." Making a concept like this part of your business culture and weaving it into your business decisions and activities will improve both your internal and external reputation. Your team will begin to think about what they do in a more holistic manner, and they will become a magnet for opportunities to become better known.

If you fully appreciate the importance of this subject, then you are halfway there. Most sound businesses can move toward improving their reputation just by making it more of a priority.

Media interest in your business. It has been said there is no such thing as bad PR. I'm not sure I believe that, but I do believe that having the media interested in your business is one of the best ways to become known and advance your brand. It also provides a morale boost for your team.

As I mentioned in the checkup, media outlets are businesses, too, and they appreciate working with companies that are good partners. Here are a few tips that may help you position your company in such a way that you gain increased media coverage.

Spread the word. If your company is doing something that will interest the media, don't keep it a secret. Send out press releases that include photographs or digital images with clear copyrights. Print media will look much more favorably on a story that includes good images that they are free to use.

Be proactive. Develop personal contacts with reporters and writers who cover your industry, and check in whenever you have something that might be of interest to talk about. Don't overdo it, though; they're busy just like you and don't have time for unscheduled calls that run longer than a few minutes. You might also include these personal contacts on mailing lists for your newsletters and marketing materials.

Consult with a PR specialist. Often a public relations specialist may want to sign you up with a retainer, but that might be overkill depending on your situation. Your primary goal is to learn what you can about dealing with the media.

Respond quickly. You don't have to drop everything when the media come calling, but returning a phone call the same day is a must. The old adage that "the early bird gets the worm" really applies in these cases. Writers who call you typically have a long list of potential sources. If they don't hear from one, they move on to the next.

Be interesting. This usually takes some practice because most company owners are not accustomed to talking in sound bites. The more specific your answers to questions are, the more of a story there is behind them, the more likely you are to be quoted.

Most media reporters, writers, and producers are always looking for an interesting story or a fresh angle on a familiar topic. It's not hard to get their attention, provided you understand that newspapers, magazines, TV, and other media outlets are businesses like any other. They make money and lose money for the same reasons you do, and they need to manage risk like any healthy business.

So, for example, just as you avoid a supplier that provides unreliable quality or service, the media avoids sources that are dishonest or that provide unreliable information. On the flipside, if you become known as a truthful, knowledgeable source, the media will return again and again to ask your opinion. Similarly, efficiency is as important to the media as it is to you. A reporter who knows that you will respond to an inquiry within twenty-four hours will call you more often because it helps her meet her deadlines.

Reputation improvement is more quantifiable than some other initiatives you may undertake. You can easily track the media clippings about your company. But the key is to plant enough seeds. Hockey great Wayne Gretsky once said, "You miss 100 percent of the shots that you never take." So get out there and take some shots.

Referrals. Everyone likes getting business referrals because they are an important source of predictable revenues. They also help to reduce marketing cost-per-lead and they are a great indicator of your reputation. All of these factors should be measured regularly to see if your "referral stock" is rising and to compare it to other businesses in your industry. Start by collecting data on past and present referrals, and making predictions about future referral targets. Use what you learn to help implement one or more of the following improvement strategies.

Create a referral culture. Begin by showing your team the importance of referrals. Reinforce the need to inspire referrals by using language that describes clients as being "delighted" or "raving fans." (Pass around a copy of books like *Raving Fans* by Ken Blanchard.)

Commit to training. Knowing how to ask for referrals may be a skill that is outside of your team's comfort zone.

Provide referral tools. For example, everyone on your team should have a business card in his or her pocket ready to hand to anyone who inquires. Our company has generated millions of dollars of business over the years by asking team members to wear company shirts with a tasteful logo.

Celebrate referrals. This will heighten interest among team members and turn them into giant radars looking for referrals.

Create incentive programs. This may sound a little desperate, but the fact is that a successful business is proud of what it does and of its product, and is always looking for opportunities to tell the company's story. Make sure you provide incentives for clients as well as team members.

All of these things bring benefits far beyond just improving your reputation, so make getting referrals a priority.

Becoming a magnet for talent. Most business owners think they have created a great place to work. They believe that they have a positive reputation and that they don't have to look for top performers because top performers come to them. But this can't be true of all of the companies making the claim, so it's one of those misconceptions that needs a closer look.

Begin by looking at the number of job applications you get when you are not actively advertising for open positions. Also look at recruitment costs over time. Survey your team to learn what they are hearing from subcontractors or vendors. And ask your colleagues at the association what the word is on the street about your business as a place to work.

The following are a few tips that you can add to your improvement to-do list to help your business shine in this area.

Leverage your team. Consider giving them incentives, which are both a nice perk and a good business investment. When you begin to deputize them, they will become more proficient at telling your story and in getting the word out on the street.

Differentiate yourself. This is Marketing 101, but it is also important when recruiting talent. Most people today yearn to join a company that stands above the pack, one they can grow with. Does your company provide opportunities for growth or just a job? Develop your own certification programs or special team experiences, and provide them with a discretionary budget.

Use the media. Your PR effort not only reinforces your brand and generates new business, it also makes your company more visible in the eyes of potential job applicants. The best talent is usually not actively reading the help wanted ads, so they need to learn about your company from print or TV media.

Many years ago after a stressful day, I came home to my family in a grumpy mood (stated mildly, I'm told). I yelled at the dog, snapped at the kids, and I wasn't very pleasant to my wife, Margie. At one point, Margie said something that I will never forget: "Mark, I wish you would just treat us like your clients." I got the immediate message, but the more I thought about her comment, the more I realized that I needed to translate this concept to how I looked at our team members. It became a top priority for me to treat them with the same reverence that I treat a client. If you are not doing the same, this one minor adjustment will lead to big improvements in how loudly your team sings your company's praises.

Legal problems. You may not have many legal problems, but do you have many adversarial situations with clients? Many of these situations are unavoidable in today's business environment, but reducing their number and frequency is a positive thing for your reputation and also your personal stress level.

The level of connectivity, primarily due to the Internet, makes every confrontation a liability that could potentially be exposed to everyone. The age of having an isolated complaint or keeping fallout from a difficult client to a minimum is gone. As essential as technology is to our business success, it can be a double-edged sword when it comes to reputation. I certainly can't keep you out of legal trouble, but I will suggest the following ways to minimize the effects.

Look for causes. Some companies adopt a "client is always right" philosophy, while others do just the reverse (usually they don't last). I encourage you to focus on why things go wrong and try to eliminate or reduce the causes. The two most common problem areas are not meeting expectations, often around quality or on-time delivery, and miscommunication. If you can instill into your team the importance of always "exceeding expectations" and always "owning" their communications, you will see a reduction in disputes and unpleasant confrontations.

Be prepared. Since it is inevitable that issues will arise, put a process in place to deal with them. It might mean passing a complaint to a supervisor or to a team member who is masterful in this area. Whatever the plan, if you have an internal process that everyone understands, you will see better results.

Act quickly. Client disputes don't solve themselves. It is important that your team addresses disputes as a top priority. Hitting these challenges quickly and proactively is the best way to minimize damage to your reputation. By acting quickly and effectively, your client will remember less about the problem and more about how you handled it.

It is difficult to generalize about client complaints, but over the years I rarely have seen an arm-wrestling match with a client that turned out in favor of the business. And rarely is there a positive outcome in court for anyone except the attorneys.

Reputation is a way of thinking. Don't underestimate its importance. At the end of your professional career, reputation is the one thing that will last forever.

Improving Stress Management

"Laughter is inner jogging."
- Norman Cousins

Up until now, the fitness elements we have discussed are reasonably easy to identify and evaluate. They are specific and concrete; they can be visualized, touched, or felt; and they can be measured. But there are other aspects of business fitness that are elusive and less tangible. Stress is one of these, and the approach to improvement in this area is more difficult because stress is both a symptom and a cause of poor business health. I believe, however, that there are processes you can follow to reduce or eliminate stress, thereby relieving the adverse effects it has on other parts of a business.

Working "on" vs. "in" your business. One of the most difficult transitions for an owner to make is from active involvement in delivery of a product or service to total focus on the systems and processes, policies, and personnel that make up the business behind the product or service. This is especially hard for business owners who evolved from the craft side, but every business owner needs strong reasons to pull back from the details and spend more time looking at the underpinnings and the big picture.

As with so many business improvements, the process begins with making a list of things you could stop doing and delegate to someone else, as well as things that you *ought* to stop doing and delegate to someone else. For each one, write a brief description of what the possible outcomes might be if you were to make the change tomorrow. Include the effects such a change would have on your clients and your team, and on your personal life. Try to imagine what your business would look like in a year or two under the new scheme. I think you will find that clients will not disappear, systems will not deteriorate, and the business will not collapse. If you have any doubts, run the idea of your pulling back by your key team members. I think you'll find them eager to step up and take on more responsibility.

Next, look at how your time is currently allocated, and try to find places where you can gain an extra twenty minutes. Usually, you can accomplish this with something simple, like shortening meeting times from sixty minutes to forty-five. If you have three meetings each week, you just gained forty-five minutes. Or consider using lunch for a mini-staff meeting. The cost of buying lunch three days a week is well worth the extra hour or two you will gain. Or try lengthening the interval between some meetings—move a once-a-week meeting to every two weeks, and you will save a couple of hours.

Another place to look is your communication habits. Screening your calls and answering voicemail might be a better use of your time than answering the phone every time it rings, no matter who is calling. Or you might switch from phone calls to e-mail or vice versa to realize greater efficiency. You may find other ways to take back a few hours each week, but the point is there generally is time to be found if you look hard enough.

These "time deposits" will add up quickly—saving just two hours each week frees up more than two weeks each year—and once you have collected a couple of hours or more, think about how to invest it. One place to start is with the massive improvement "to-do" you've built by reading this book. Earlier I mentioned a simple technique that has helped me: making a regular appointment with yourself, like you would with any client. Just setting aside time devoted entirely to your own agenda will reduce your stress level. A scheduled appointment eliminates the time pressure and removes the need to rush through one task to make sure you have enough for the next. Begin with just a couple of hours a week, then increase it over time.

You will be more effective with this newfound planning time if you set the right atmosphere. In an appointment with a client, you don't let your phone or a team member interrupt you; the same applies to meetings you schedule for yourself. If you still feel that you are not putting this time to best use, try using a different location—your home or a restaurant. It is critical that you find a place where you can really focus and think about important business issues.

As you begin to develop ideas and actions to improve your business, make follow-up appointments to yourself. Monitoring your progress not only makes you accountable to the business but also helps to make sure these new habits stick.

Proactive vs. reactive. Lack of control creates stress, and many business people have far less control over their day than they imagine.

Ask yourself what percentage of your day is reactive—that is, spent addressing crises or conducting unplanned interventions—and what percentage is proactive—deliberately planned or part of a predictable routine. Results vary, but a good rule of thumb is if you are spending more then 20 percent of your day in a reactive mode, you need to work on taking control of your time. Fortunately, most people can make a quick change in their level by making a few simple fixes.

If you have a client-based business, you may have a handful of clients whose frequent demands are a major source of interruptions. The solution is to shift to a more proactive approach. Instead of waiting for something to prompt them to call you, take the initiative and call them first. Every Monday morning—Monday is a good day to do this because the whole week lies ahead—contact five clients who are routine sources of interruptions that put you into reactive mode and ask them what their needs may be that week. Then set a time when you can call them back or visit with them to catch up and resolve their issues. Even if only three of the five make it on to your agenda, you will have shifted 60 percent of your interactions with them from the reactive column into the proactive column. You still have to spend the time, but it is at your convenience, at a time when it does the least damage to other activities on your schedule.

Another major source of reactive time is your team. It could be someone who buttonholes you unexpectedly in the hall or barges into your office with a question. Some of these interruptions are inevitable and the result of an open-door management policy. But unless these encounters are truly brief—a minute or less—they can put a kink into your day. Next time this happens, try saying something like this: "Bob, this sounds like something that will take some time to resolve. Let's sit down later today and talk it through." But don't stop there: make an appointment for a specific time and duration. Just like that you have shifted an interruption into a planned meeting and transformed "accidental" reactive time into scheduled proactive time.

The benefits of gaining control of your time in this way will soon appear. You will experience less stress, accomplish more, think more clearly, address medium- and long-term issues more effectively, and keep promises with others more easily. And when you begin to feel the benefits, you will come up with other ways to increase your proactive time.

Limiting your hours. Whether you or your key team members limit the number of hours they invest into the business is not the central issue when it comes to stress management. The question is: Do you have a choice? Many business people are hardworking and put in a lot of hours, but much of that effort is wasted because it is spent scrambling to quell crises or jumping from one emergency to the next. It is not really their choice to work so hard; they are compelled to do it by events that are out of their control. The result is less effective output and high levels of stress.

Most business people cannot accurately estimate the amount of time they spend in a typical workday, so the first step is to find out just what the situation is in your case. Keep a simple written timesheet that you fill out each day for a week (longer is even better). Make notes to describe how you spent the time. Chances are you'll be surprised by the results, which will likely be a larger number of hours than you would have guessed. Next, decide which activities can be delegated immediately and which might eventually be taken over by someone who could be trained to do the work. This won't necessarily be easy to do, particularly if, like many business owners, you believe that there are certain things that you do better than anyone else. Whether or not that's true isn't the issue; you will never gain control of your time until you decide what you can take off your plate and transfer to someone else.

I like to quantify time because it motivates me to find time. For example, finding just twenty minutes per day for one month is a gift of more than a day. Over the course of a year it is about two-and-a-half weeks. Imagine what you could do with an extra two-and-a-half weeks, professionally or personally, then write it down and treat it as a goal. It will help you find the discipline to make time matter.

Also challenge yourself to do things in a shorter amount of time. Work expands to fill the available time. If you shorten the amount of time available, generally the work still gets done—and you get back the time you saved.

Aggressive but realistic. As I have mentioned in earlier chapters, finding the right pace will dramatically affect both results and the levels of stress generated to achieve them. I try to balance an aggressive pace with what is realistically achievable. This "aggressive but realistic" test is one to which I subject all plans and all expectations.

Improvement in stress management is best achieved in baby steps. Be patient, and whatever you do, don't let your efforts in this direction create even more stress. Focus first on the simplest, most obvious actions. This will lead to immediate gains that will provide some of the relief you need to take on more challenging changes .

Improving Positioning

"It never gets easier, you just go faster."
- Greg LeMond

A well-positioned business is well rounded, solid, and balanced. We feel confident that this business will grow bigger and better years from now. As you try to better understand positioning, keep in mind that although improvement in this area is a long-term proposition, the effects of being well positioned have positive short-term benefits as well.

Stable and consistent. As we discussed in the fitness checkup, being stable and consistent lowers risk and gives you a strong foundation on which to build improvements. Stability also creates the confidence needed to make business decisions with conviction and clarity. Improving your stability begins with a serious examination of three primary key areas for every business: product, processes, and people. All three of these are folded into other areas of our fitness criteria, but try to filter each one for stability and consistency.

Beginning with product, ask questions like these: "Is the product or service you deliver consistent in quality and client experience? Is our product stable and can it stand up to the competition and a changing business environment?" The answers will be subjective, so test them against those of a few key team members.

With regard to processes, does your process deliver a predictable outcome? Are your processes delivering an enhanced client experience, or are they limited to internal benefits? Which processes meet this test and which don't?

Team consistency is about playing by the same rules and being clear about accountability. Some individuals with high marks in this area may not be your top guns or all-star players, but their stabilizing influence provides good balance.

Communicate the results to the rest of your team. The more they understand the importance of stability and consistency, the more they will rally behind your findings.

Strong market awareness. Well-positioned businesses are sensitive to changes in the market. They have their ears to the ground and are light of foot. They are responding to both external and internal inputs.

One way to make this broad topic seem more manageable is to put different aspects of market awareness into different "buckets." Most obvious are market forces acting through your clients, your geographical location, and your marketing strategies. Your business is also affected by fluctuations in the regulatory climate and in the price and availability of raw materials. A third bucket of market awareness is with your team. Understanding generational differences, availability of talent, and training requirements will have a dramatic effect on how well positioned you are both now and in the future.

Something that we did in our business many years ago illustrates what I mean perfectly. At the time we had a main office in Maryland about equidistant from the borders of Washington, D.C., and Virginia. While looking over our revenue statements, we realized that only about five percent of our business was coming from Virginia, even though the market opportunity was about the same in all three areas. After gathering some more information, we discovered that Virginia homeowners preferred to do business with companies located in Virginia. Within a year of opening a very small office in Virginia, we increased the volume of Virginia-based business to about 25 percent, five times what it had been.

Getting an outside perspective on these elements can be very helpful to your business. You might want to assemble a few key team members for a brainstorming session. For each of the market inputs mentioned above, describe what the situation was three years ago, what it is now, and what you think it will be like three years from now.

When the list is complete, try to determine in which areas you are better positioned for the future than you were three years ago, and where you are not. Invest some time fixing the "now" but with an eye toward how those changes will affect your company three years from now. For example, in our remodeling business, the recent boom years brought with it a shortage of skilled labor. Currently, however, the market has cooled down a bit and there is not enough work to go around, creating an abundance of skilled labor. Looking ahead a year or two, business is likely to be booming again. Knowing all of this, we have decided that now is a good time to recruit skilled labor. Making the investment isn't easy in a slow market, but the opportunity won't be here for long.

Well capitalized. It is not my intention to tell you how much capital you need or where to find it, but I do want you to think about what it means to be well capitalized. If you understand your numbers, have a strong handle on cash flow, and can predict profitability, you may be able to determine the answer on your own. But if you struggle in any of these areas, bring in your accountant or a business advisor to help you.

Begin the analysis with some negative "what if" scenarios. What if you missed your sales projections by 20 to 30 percent for three to six months? What if a couple of clients delayed or withheld payment? What if you were locked into several contracts and you suddenly experience major price increases from your vendors? In each case, try to determine what the effect would be on cash flow, then check to see if you have—or can easily obtain—the capital to meet the need.

Proper capitalization isn't merely a hedge against a negative turn of events, it also supports positive changes. What if, for example, you suddenly had an opportunity to invest into some real estate to move your office? What if a small competitor were to come to you with an offer to sell his business? Would you have the capital to take advantage of these kinds of opportunities?

The best time to borrow money or set up lines of credit is when you don't need it. Think about the lender's perspective. Lenders are much more likely to be interested in loaning money to or setting up a line of credit with a company that has a flush bank account than with one that is feeling the pinch and scrambling to pay its bills.

But banks aren't the only source of capital. You may have friends or family who would consider investing in your company, particularly to help you take advantage of a unique opportunity. Like the bank, they would rather invest when you are solvent, not when you are desperate. Discussing the issue with them early helps. Just knowing that you have access to capital should you need it will build confidence and influence your business decisions.

I am not aware of any businesses that did not need to borrow money at one point or another. Create a plan now to gain access to the funds you need, and you will be much better positioned for any circumstance.

Diversified for risk. Think about your business as an investment portfolio. Are all of your eggs in one basket? Are you relying too heavily on a strong upward trend without considering how long it will last? What goes up generally comes back down, and it's difficult to know when or how fast circumstances might change. Being diversified can act as a hedge against these kinds of changes.

Plan carefully before you diversify, however, because it is a double-edged sword. The positive aspect is that in a down market, you may be able to reduce your risk. This will keep you from losing some of the ground or market share you gained in an up market. The downside is that diversification takes corporate energy. It dilutes your focus and it can create conflicts among business models that might be difficult to reconcile.

In the case of our business, diversification grew out of necessity. In the early 1990s, a lull in the real estate market caused home appreciation to stall or even reverse itself. The result was a 50 percent drop in our business, which at the time was focused entirely on larger-scale residential remodeling projects. We quickly realized that our present and future business was determined by a single product and service that was completely tied to fluctuations in the housing market. We also recognized, however, a strong demand for small-scale projects and eventually opened our handyman division. This business model not only complemented our large-project remodeling services by enabling us to serve the repair needs of past clients, but it also added new clients to our database who might need larger-scale projects when the economy rebounded.

Although the handyman business made sense on paper, it required a tremendous investment in time and money to develop new systems and processes. In the end, however, it brought stability in down markets, created opportunities for local growth, and eventually led to our developing a national franchise operation.

There are generally two ways to diversify, horizontally or vertically. When you diversify horizontally, you widen your geographic reach or increase the size of the market you can do business with. In other words, you can expand to cover a thirty-mile radius instead of a fifteen-mile radius, or you can open a second location to be able to handle more of the same types of customers in the same area. You might even acquire another business to accomplish horizontal diversification.

Diversifying vertically involves taking your existing product to a new client. For example, you might begin to offer what began as residential handyman services to a commercial market.

As you take inventory of your present business fitness, you need to at least explore these options so that when the time is right you can act. If you are properly positioned then you can turn up the faucet when the market shifts and the opportunity speaks to you.

Investing in the future. When we think about investments, we think about money, but you can leave your wallet in your pocket. An investment of time is just as fruitful when it comes to improving your positioning.

Start by investing one to two hours each week imagining what the future might look like. Better define what growth means for your company. Look in the mirror and ask what the next steps might be for you, personally and professionally, and ask the same about key team members. Who will take your position and allow you to move forward and grow? Is this person able to move into your shoes now? If not, why not, and what would be required to get him or her there? Investing time in future leaders is critical to good business positioning. Over the years, I have at times spent as much as half of my time and energy in this area.

Also examine your product or service. Will your clients be as enthusiastic about what you are providing in the future as they are now? What about the way you deliver it?

Being well positioned is the outcome of the effort you expend now focusing on specific aspects of your business. It is a never-ending process that will get easier as your business becomes healthier. Eventually, thinking about your business's positioning will become second nature.

Improving Alliances

"Individual commitment to a group effort – that is what makes a team work, a company work, a society work, a civilization work."
- Vince Lombardi

Next to technology, strategic alliances will probably have the most influence on the way you do business in the future. As the world has gotten smaller and more connected, business has become more complex, and one person's success is dramatically affected by others. Improvement in this area is not very difficult but does require a conscious effort to see and understand these interconnections and use them to your advantage.

Establishing alliances. When I was in my early twenties, I designed and built a home in a remote area of the mountains. I would spend several days alone working on the house. On some trips, I would never see another human being. I got the work done, but I had no one to bounce ideas off of, no one to help find solutions. True, I learned a lot about self-reliance, but I also came to appreciate the importance of the skills and perspective of other people. This is as true in our business lives as it is in our personal lives.

You probably know business people who have a deep network of relationships. It may seem from your vantage point that they have some innate ability to build friendships or that they are lucky to be in the right place at the right time. In some cases, you might be right, but I have found that most of the time, these people build networks because they believe the networks are important, and they focus time and energy on building and maintaining them.

Improvement in this area begins with your mindset. The ability to build relationships is not a natural talent; it is a product of deliberate effort. Start by making a list of a few existing relationships that could be enhanced. Don't overcomplicate this one—it is truly an example of how little things can and do indeed matter.

For instance, I have a financial advisor whose techniques for keeping in touch with me are impressive. He not only calls me regularly, but he also sends me a handwritten note on my birthday, forwards articles that may be of interest to me personally or professionally, and always follows up on any little personal comment I may have made concerning almost any subject. Coupled with his skill as an advisor, this kind of attention has enhanced our relationship and converted me into a very loyal client. I have reciprocated by inviting him to share his ideas about relationship building with our sales teams. His talk not only benefited the group but introduced him to a few new clients as well.

The next step is to list some other possible businesses that may create a positive alliance in the future. It may help if you and key team members engage in more interactions outside of a strict working schedule by joining an association or networking group. By investing a couple of hours a week with a new circle of people, you will increase the universe of potential alliances dramatically. This process may take years, but the benefits will last long beyond that.

Regular dialogue and communication. It is hard to expand your universe of friends or even maintain the ones you presently have if you don't have some regular communication with them. In business, having a dialogue is where the benefits lie. Improving in this area is simple, but it does require a little discipline. If your time is extremely limited, begin with calling one old ally and one new ally each week. As I've suggested in other contexts, put these appointments on your calendar and treat them as you would any other commitment. Keep the conversation brief, but make a point to discuss issues beyond the day-to-day projects, such as where they see their biggest growth opportunities or what they may be seeing in the marketplace. After each call, if appropriate, make a commitment to a follow-up call or even a face-to-face meeting in the future.

Another way to become more proactive in this area is to set up a breakfast or lunch with a group of professional friends. This is an efficient way to leverage your time and gain loyalty from allies.

As these relationships evolve, you will see ideas start to pop. Your alliances will become your eyes and ears in the marketplace, helping you recruit new team members or evaluate positioning. They can also become excellent market awareness and intelligence tools that increase your opportunities and help you avoid pitfalls. You might also use them as a sounding board or advisory group as you grow your operation.

Synergistic opportunities. As you begin to communicate more frequently with business alliances, it is only natural to begin to look for synergistic opportunities. These are ideas that benefit both of the parties involved. One way to find places where synergies might lie is to discuss win-win opportunities with your alliances. Make a list with two columns, one for your business and one for theirs (you can do this on your own or in a meeting with the business involved). In each column, list goals for the relationship, then see where the lists complement each other.

For example, a few years ago we were looking for ways to expand the awareness of our brand, while a large manufacturer we work with was trying to create loyalty with its clients. We decided to conduct a series of business seminars to which they would invite their clients, a solution that helped both parties reach their goals.

After you have completed this exercise, map out a simple plan to put your toe in the water. Since you each have independent businesses, begin with some modest tests. If these pilots prove to be successful then move them into more involved synergistic opportunities.

It takes a real commitment and some discipline to keep all of the day-to-day distractions from getting in the way of success. If a pilot does not work out, go back and ask why. You may find you missed the mark on some details or some cultural disconnects, or that you were unrealistic in your expectations and goals. Occasionally, it may be that you were working with the wrong ally. Don't be discouraged. You will find your alliance fitness score will improve if you make a conscious effort and invest a little time.

Making It Happen

"Don't let what you can not do interfere with what you can do."
- John Wooden

One common denominator of healthy and fit businesses is a commitment to constant improvement. When constant improvement becomes a way of life, it becomes less overwhelming and painful. It becomes the lens through which a business looks at itself, and a way of approaching everything it does.

Embracing improvement is a matter of adopting a new mindset. In many cases, it will also mean instigating a major cultural shift within your company. These changes are as important to business health as the individual steps to improvement themselves.

By now you have probably accumulated a massive improvement "to-do" list and are struggling with the feeling of being overwhelmed. Here are some tips to help you figure out where to start and how to build momentum.

"Rome was not built in a day." Although your improvement regimen will progress one small step at a time, it's important to be able to see the big picture right from the start. Make a list of all of the improvement opportunities you identified as you read through the second half of the book. Include everything, no matter how ill-defined it is in your mind, or even if it is something that you know you can fix immediately. Include items even for which you can only identify an issue but not a resolution—answers will come later so long as you ask the right questions. You may want to go back and review your original fitness checkup to see if the way you scored yourself is still accurate. And if you have other team members participating in this book's process, ask them to review it and add to the list.

For now, organize the list using the fitness checkup chapters; you can always reorganize it later. This list is your blueprint for improvement, your roadmap to business health, and you will be consulting it for a long time to come. Try to create as complete a list as possible, but don't worry about leaving something out; you will find yourself adding, changing, and deleting items on the list on a regular basis.

"Aggressive but realistic." Once you have built your master list, review it with an eye toward prioritizing it. Try to group similar tasks together. For example, if you find that you need to consult an accountant for three specific objectives, group these together and plan to address all three issues in a single meeting. When you have the list of tasks reorganized and regrouped, pick three fitness keys that you think need the most immediate attention.

This shorter list is where you will focus your attention. Devise a plan that spells out what steps you will take to improve, when you will start to make the changes, who will take responsibility for implementing and monitoring the changes, and when you think the overall improvement goal should be reached. Before you get too far along, solicit feedback from other team members. Depending on your company, you could accomplish this by organizing a dedicated planning meeting, or you could simply raise these issues at a regularly scheduled meeting. You might want to create a special weekly or monthly communication on the improvement initiative or you may simply incorporate updates into your established communication network. However you approach it, the important thing is to get buy-in early from your team, especially from those in key positions who will be responsible for implementing some of the changes and for ensuring that the plan is adopted further down the line.

Planning is a skill like any other. If you don't feel up to the task, even with help from team members, consider hiring an advisor or consultant to assist you. Any additional expense will be returned to you many times over if the instruction and assistance succeeds in moving your company a notch closer to better fitness.

As we discussed in earlier chapters, finding the right cadence for business improvements can be as challenging as making the changes themselves. Keep in mind the "aggressive but realistic" approach and use it to help communicate your goals to your team. Remember, your planning process should address not only what you plan to do but also the effect those actions will have on others and on their perception of the overall process. Plan thoroughly, and launch the plan only when you believe the stage has been properly set. A false start is not disastrous, but will make it more difficult to regain momentum and team commitment.

Managing change. Managers can effectively execute the plan that you develop, but it takes leadership to ensure that everyone adopts the plan and becomes a part of company culture.

It is easy to underestimate the importance of strong leadership in an undertaking of this magnitude. Business leaders are often so close to an idea that they can't imagine why anyone would not jump on board without a second thought. But instituting the kind of changes that this checkup promotes is not a trivial matter. The improvement plan will make the jobs of some team members more difficult and in other cases it will merely be perceived to have done so. Either way, the resulting resistance has the same effect and creates a drag on the entire effort. It is very much like what often happens when parents assume that their children will be delighted by a trip they have planned. The destination sounds attractive enough, but as soon as they hit the road, the kids start complaining about other things they would rather be doing, how long it is taking to get there, and how they need to stop to buy snacks or other things they need to endure the journey. Suddenly, the well-intended family outing is not so much fun for anyone.

Your team is your family, and managing their reaction and dedication to the improvement plan involves a creative approach, frequent interaction, extensive communication, and plenty of empathy. Always be aware that your team will react to the improvement plan in very different ways. Some will embrace change easily; others may like the ideas but find change painful and overwhelming. Some will be immediately enthusiastic, while others appear apathetic. As mentioned earlier, try not to judge them personally by their reactions. Instead, anticipate the variety of reactions and try to accommodate them all. Try to stay positive and keep an open mind while at the same time sticking to your commitment to improve. When the going gets rough, remember that the benefits your business will ultimately reap when the improvements are achieved will be well worth the effort invested along the way.

Fitness Checkup Follow-Up

"I don't think much of a man who is not wiser
today than he was yesterday."
- Abraham Lincoln

The last thing a doctor or dentist will advise you to do after a checkup is to make an appointment for a follow-up checkup. How soon you need to make the appointment and how long it will last depends on the results of the checkup, the need to monitor progress, and the doctor's desire to make you accountable for whatever fitness regimen you have agreed to undertake. If your dentist finds a cavity, she may want you to return in two weeks or even sooner; if there is merely the potential for a cavity, however, she may not need you to schedule a visit for six months; and if everything looks great, she may not want to see you for a year. It could also be that the checkup uncovers a condition that prompts the dentist to refer you to a specialist, whose evaluation is necessary before anything further can be done.

When applied to our physical well-being, everyone comprehends the importance of a follow-up. Often we have felt the pain of not following up, and so the process has become second nature to us. One could argue that the follow-up appointment is as important to us as the initial visit itself. The concept of a follow-up applies equally well to your business but, unlike with the dentist, you have not grown up with an annual business checkup. And although you know plenty of people who visit the dentist regularly, it is likely that you don't know anyone who performs a regular business checkup, so you don't have any role models to emulate.

This book can fill that gap. If you have skimmed the book and completed some but not all of the exercises, you may want to make a note on your calendar to reread it in six months. We all act to improve ourselves when we are ready. Acting too soon, before you or your team is ready, will make progress that much harder.

If you have read this book all the way through and completed all of the exercises, then you are ready to design and implement an improvement plan, and the follow-up interval will depend on your fitness results. The daily, weekly, and monthly action items in your improvement plan will serve as a guide to how soon you need to repeat the checkup. It may be that you will return in six months and repeat the checkup for only those fitness keys in which you have implemented changes. How useful the follow-up will be depends on how specific and measurable your actions are. For example, a plan to "improve the sales team" is not as specific and measurable as "improve the sales team's close rate from 20 to 25 percent by next quarter, and increase the number of client visits from five to seven per week."

Some improvement steps are less quantifiable, however. For instance, you might want to improve the attitude of the sales team so they can better cope with a tough market condition. The approach you take may be something as simple as popping into the sales meeting to offer a few encouraging words. Or you might make a deliberate effort to chat with individual salespeople in the hall or at the coffee machine where you can listen to their challenges and offer advice in a more informal way. Measuring the change in their attitude may be hard to do, but you can still write down the objective and schedule time for it. When it comes time to review progress, your gut will tell you if you are heading in the right direction.

Many years ago, I created what I thought was a wonderful improvement plan and launched it with a great deal of enthusiasm and passion. The plan worked well for a couple of weeks, and then gradually petered out until one or two months into the process we were already out of gas. Since then, I have tried several alternative ways to implement improvement plans, and have developed some techniques that work very well for our business. If you are able to adapt them to your planning and follow-up process, I think they will work well for you, too.

First, short-term actions should be specific and implemented and reviewed in short cycles. I have found that 3 is a magic number. If you try to break down and limit your priorities to three, you are more likely to succeed.

We have already discussed prioritizing your to-do lists and targeting three fitness keys for immediate improvements. Following the rule of threes, create three actions steps for each key. Write these down and post the list in a place where you can see them first thing every morning. (I stick mine on the side of my computer screen.) Then, make a weekly appointment with yourself to spend thirty minutes reflecting on and monitoring your progress in each of the nine steps. Once a month, spend two or three hours taking inventory of progress made and adjust your course as necessary for the upcoming month. Once each quarter, (another interval based on the magic number 3—three months), set aside even more time—a half-day or more, possibly offsite—to really think through what about the improvement process is working and what is not. Use this time to determine if anything in your thinking or the environment has changed that might have knocked your plan off track. Pick up this book again and refresh yourself on a specific fitness key to discover if your scores have improved or declined.

On the anniversary of your original fitness checkup, it is time to come back to the "doctor"—the fitness checkup—for a complete examination. Reread the entire book; you will find that your changed circumstances will give you a fresh perspective on the material and that you will latch on to new insights. Take the test again, but don't look at last year's scores until afterwards. Bring those who participated the first time back into the process, and consider inviting someone new. Once you have a new set of checkup results, compare them with the previous year's results. It is always good when what you discover is that scores in your targeted fitness keys have improved or that your overall score has improved, but that won't always be the case. It's perfectly normal for some scores to have slipped a bit; in fact, it is not unusual to find that your overall score has slipped a little. This does not mean your business is less fit than it was a year ago, but it does indicate that something has changed. Very possibly it is an indication that you understand the test questions a bit more thoroughly than you did the first time through. It may also be that your circumstances have changed, volume has grown, or you have changed vendors or entered into a new market, all of which will affect some of your scores. Or it could simply be that the changes you are implementing require that you move one step back before you can move forward. Naturally, you wouldn't want this situation to persist, but it is not uncommon for businesses to see these kinds of changes in their fitness score in the first year.

Treat this process as a journey, not a destination. Although they are often confused, reaching traditional business milestones and becoming healthier are two separate outcomes. Success in both our business and personal lives is a blend of the mindset, healthy behavior, and the results. Without the right success habits, achieving sustainable positive results is impossible.

Epilogue

"We don't stop playing because we grow old; we grow old because we stop playing."
- George Bernard Shaw

For those readers who are exhausted from making business "to do" lists, you can finally set your pen down while I attempt to tie a bow around what I have tried to achieve with this book.

I have chosen to point out the parallels between personal health and fitness and business success not because the analogy is perfect, and only partly because of my successful experience with a weight-loss system that I chanced upon one morning many years ago while flipping through TV channels. I chose to compare business fitness to physical fitness because our personal health is something we all understand from an early age. Although physical health is infinitely complex, the concept of physical fitness itself is simple. Its language and concepts are familiar to us, and we can apply its lessons to business more readily than other common experiences. I chose the metaphor of physical fitness because I wanted the business ideas to stick so that you might be

213

able to see your business from a different angle and realize that, like an athlete in training, you can improve and become fit.

If I have succeeded, then the next time you are seated in a restaurant listening to the waiter, you will begin to draw parallels to your business. If I have succeeded, then the next time you attend a sporting event you will think about the coach not merely as a playmaker but as a leader and team builder, just like you. And certainly, if I have been successful, the next time you visit your doctor you will have a different perspective on everything he or she says and does, and doesn't say and doesn't do.

In a word, you will begin to see the world through the lens of your business, and how you see things affects how meaningful they are. Most successful businesspeople are optimists; they have an uncanny ability to always see the glass as half full, not half empty. They can extract meaning and benefit from almost any situation because they are committed to improvement. They can celebrate the wins but never take their eye off tomorrow and the next challenge. They love to get a "no" because it helps them get to the "yes."

I know that this all sounds a little corny and trite, but that doesn't make it any less true. Businesspeople understand better than almost anyone that success is not the result of outside influences or inevitable circumstances; it comes from within. Success depends on your perspective, your commitment to developing the required skills, from your passion and enthusiasm, and from focusing on the right things at the right time. Success comes from keeping the short and long term in balance, from taking appropriate risks and getting out of your comfort zone, from your empathy and commitment to others. For most of us, the revelation that we are in control of our destiny makes true freedom and happiness possible.

I hope that throughout this book, I have served you well as tour guide and a part-time therapist. I hope also that this book is not the end of your exploration but rather the first leg of an otherwise long and wonderful journey. It has certainly been that for me. I have taught these concepts for years to all sorts of business groups in a variety of settings, but putting it in writing has been an extraordinary experience for me. There is an old saying that he who teaches learns twice. Thank you for the opportunity to share these ideas, and in the teaching to find the lesson.

–Mark Richardson

About the Author

Mark Richardson's involvement in design and business spans more than three decades. A graduate of the School of Architecture at Virginia Tech, his career has been defined by his leadership and entrepreneurial spirit. As the President of Case, he has led its growth of over 1000% by expanding services and market reach. For ten years he hosted *"At Home with Mark Richardson,"* a weekly radio show dedicated to bringing a slice of the remodeling industry to consumers and business practitioners alike.

Mark is a guest lecturer for MBA Programs at Virginia Tech, Georgetown University and the University of Maryland. He serves as a business advisor to many business sectors from small practices to major corporations. In 2007 he developed with The Home Depot a series of online business workshops designed to offer professionals effective and intelligent business practices from business fitness to sales and marketing strategies. Mark sits on many advisory boards including Harvard University's Joint Center for Housing Studies, GE Money, and the Better Business Bureau of Greater Washington. He is a monthly columnist for Remodeling Magazine and Smart Business Ideas. Other Mark Richardson vehicles include: *Thirty Day Remodeling Fitness Program* and *The Remodeling Live Series.* In 2008 Mark was inducted into the National Association of Home Builders Hall of Fame.

Mark is the President of Case Institute of Remodeling, an educational/knowledge hub for the construction/remodeling industry. For more information visit:

www.caseinstituteofremodeling.com

For questions and insight about Mark or to access articles, teleconferences, speaking opportunities and seminars, contact him via E-mail at **mrichardson@casedesign.com** or by phone at **301-229-9580**.

For More Information visit:
www.casedesign.com and **www.caseremodeling.com**